CRITICISM
FRIEND *or* FOE?

CRITICISM
FRIEND *or* FOE?

DOUG MURREN

published by
AMG *Publishers*

Criticism: Friend or Foe?

Copyright © 2003 by Doug Murren
Published by AMG Publishers
6815 Shallowford Rd.
Chattanooga, Tennessee 37421

ISBN 0-89957-133-6

First printing—July 2003

Cover designed by ImageWright, Inc., Chattanooga, Tennessee
Interior design and typesetting by Reider Publishing Services,
    West Hollywood, California
Edited and Proofread by Jonathan Wright, Dan Penwell, Sharon Neal,
    and Warren Baker

Printed in the United States of America
09 08 07 06 05 04 03 –RO– 8 7 6 5 4 3 2 1

To my mother and father for their devotion to me, their devotion to my family, and their devotion to Christ. I could not have faced life without their support—time, after time, after time.

Thanks, Mom and Dad.

Contents

Preface

I'M LEARNING at fifty years of age to understand the real value of criticism. I've been a church leader for over thirty years so I know all about criticism. I definitely know what it feels like.

I hate being criticized, and I don't know anyone who enjoys it. Yet we all face it, and we all give it, but it's dangerous ground. Jesus warned as much about rendering wrongful judgment as almost any other topic. He knew how touchy and treacherous human relationships could become.

The fascinating thing about criticism is that we get as much as we give in the manner that we give it. That is why I have written this book. The skill is woefully thin on how to do criticism.

I didn't really plan to write this book but my agent, Bruce Barbour, read a brief outline in a weekly email newsletter I write on: "How Leaders Can Handle Criticism." He asked me if I could put it in book form, so I did just that. And this book is the outcome.

I've reviewed the matters of criticism from different vantage points to allow the material to sink in deep. The book is designed to be a tool not only for all Christians, but also for church boards and parents as well.

I hope this book will be a regular friend on your journey in the days ahead.

Introduction

CRITICISM CAN be a friend. It can also be a deadly foe. Learning to tell the difference can make life a much happier journey. This book is about learning to tell the difference between the two.

Christians who don't learn to receive correction will remain muddled in immaturity, but learning to receive correction is not an innate ability. Our innate ability is to reject correction. Learning to hear life-giving criticism takes a good deal of practice. The Bible affirms that none of us can afford to reject criticism and expect to succeed at life.

Learning to hear the criticism that we'd prefer not to hear is the main road to maturity. If we don't take this path we run the risk of living in a fantasy world with no connection to reality. And fantasies cripple the possessor.

If we don't give healthy criticism, can we claim to love others as Christ loved us? The Bible encourages us to learn to criticize with a love that can rescue family, friends, and fellow Christians. Criticism is a necessary gift for giver and receiver and is a topic that demands sober attention.

Joyous Reality or Destructive Lies

Since Adam and Eve's last walk through the garden men and women have been hiding from reality. We spend great amounts of energy trying to avoid criticism. We dread the moments of scrutiny. The bushes we hide behind include denial, anger, and judgment as we hope to turn the light off ourselves and onto others.

Criticism sits and waits at our doorstep every day of our lives saying, "Hey, let me introduce you to the real you. Let me hold a mirror up for you to see how you really act." Criticism keeps us from hiding our faults.

Criticism triggers fear in our broken hearts before it inspires joy. One of our first impulses when criticized is to run and hide. We run because we hate the embarrassment of rejection and the reality of imperfection, but, truth be known, no one ever hides anything. We need healing of our fears to face life successfully.

Yes, we resist correction and we do it well. But spiritual growth requires that we come out of hiding. This never happens without the help of what I call witnesses. Witnesses are observers who hold up mirrors allowing us to judge ourselves. Witnesses give evidence to us as to what reality is. Their tool is loving criticism. The critical question is will we listen or run? Will we accept the correction or hide?

I helped a well-known NBA basketball player in the 1980s beat a cocaine habit. He was remanded into my custody on two conditions: First, I would be responsible to keep him away from the bad parts of town. Second, he would go through rehab for his drug problem. My friend followed both guidelines for six months, but then during the seventh month I got a frantic call from his wife.

"Steve is in the basement bathroom freebasing cocaine (smoking the drug with a pipe) and he won't come out."

Upon hearing the news I jumped in my car and headed to Steve's house. Sure enough, I found my friend locked in the bathroom. Finally his wife found a key, and I unlocked the door quietly and burst in. There was Steve standing in the middle of the small bathroom with the pipe in hand.

"Steve, what are you doing?" I blurted out.

"I was just seeing if I would take it or not," he said.

I looked around at the black tar on the floor and said, "Well, it looks like you did take quite a bit."

He responded, "I was just lighting it up and showing myself I wouldn't inhale."

Steve is an example of humankind's ability to deny sinful behavior. We would rather deny or run and hide than face the truth. But a loving God's amazing grace is ready to forgive despite our imperfections. Once we understand God's grace, we're more likely to embrace correction as a friend.

We all need help to find our way to mental, social, and spiritual health. The fact we need this help is why Christians gather in communities. Paul taught the church in Galatia that they were to restore a fellow Christian when he or she was caught in a fault. They were to restore the fallen believer with kindness and gentleness remembering that they also might need similar help in the future (see Gal. 6).

Criticism never feels right at first. My initial reaction to criticism is denial. I know few people who ask friends and acquaintances, "Hey, could you do a critique on my life? I need a jolt back to reality today." I grow closer to reality when I silence my fears, come out of hiding, and embrace the real me. But why do I have such a difficult time remembering this lesson? Because criticism is a friend, but our taste for it must grow. Just when I think I have made a friend of criticism, I find myself denying it, becoming angry, or blaming someone else.

Criticism and a Story with a Happy Ending

A few years ago I was called to be the confessor for a lay leader, that I'll call Jim. His story shows the positive power of a friend's rebuke. Jim was highly esteemed in his community. He had a strong grasp of the Bible, generated instant respect as soon as you'd meet him, and was the chairman of the church board. His business had done well for years, but the stress of working too many hours had encroached on his home life. Painful tension between him and his wife was continuing to grow. They seldom talked to each other, even though they both shared a passion for the church.

Jim had set up a romantic rendezvous with an employee's wife a few weeks before my visit, but the tryst never took place. He made a decision that night to renew his commitment to his wife. Jim lived several weeks with intense shame before we got together and talked. He had been reluctant to seek help from his pastor, or anyone he knew, for fear of being rejected.

A partner in Jim's office confronted him two days before I arrived and urged him to get help. He told Jim that he could lose it all and that Jim must do whatever was necessary to protect his family and his testimony.

The second day at the church Jim took me to see his factory. We walked around the large warehouse talking about church business and our kids. It was then he began to cry.

"Doug," He said. "I want to get my life back on track. I'm way off course. I feel sick to the very core of my heart."

He proceeded to tell me of the damaged relationship and the struggles he was having at home. Jim didn't withhold any of the truth from me. He became his own critic that night, and I became an ally in his journey back to spiritual health. He made that trek that we all must make at some point in our lives—from lies to the truth. He hugged the truth that night.

He asked me, "How can I get back on course and stay on course?"

"You need people who know and love you enough to confront you and drive you to honesty," was my response. "Your wife needs to be invited deeper into your heart and allowed to assess your growth."

He asked if I would meet confidentially with him and his wife. I did meet with them the next evening. Jim was surprised when his wife confessed her long-standing bitterness and anger. Jim and his wife committed, that night, to break the years of compounded criticism and dissatisfaction they had for one another. They listened to each other with open hearts, and the truth set them free as their path turned in a hopeful direction. Both had feared discovery and both had hidden in denial for years with smiles on their faces.

Friendly Observers

The fear of being caught is all around us. It drives people to interpersonal warfare within homes and offices. Denial is the most sophisticated response. My children began their denial as toddlers saying, "No I didn't do it." Their response was a sure sign of guilt.

I cringe with embarrassment as I remember my children telling their friends about my shortcomings. They were acute observers of my life. Often they were used by God to help me become the father I wanted to be. God has inventive ways to help us face reality.

I'm not sure whether my friend Jim would have come to himself if it hadn't been for his partner and his willingness to confront him. It's likely Jim would have fallen further into his depression if his friend hadn't been there. Whether he could have found his way out of the deep mire is highly questionable. We all need friends who will confront us—like Jim's friend.

Unexpected Critics

Even dreaming seems to bring correction our way. King Nebuchadnezzar in the book of Daniel had an interesting dream that revealed his presumptuous pride. Daniel revealed the meaning of the dream— God was going to correct the king for calling himself a god. He warned the king that when a man's own dreams criticize him, it's time to face reality.

I chuckle about a dream I've had numerous times. I'm in a crowded sixth grade classroom and I'm seated at my desk with nothing on but my underwear. Yet, in the dream, no one notices my scant attire. I spend what seems like days trying to figure how I can escape without my classmates noticing my meager garment. Then the dream ends.

I have asked many groups if others have had this dream. Many acknowledge they have. We experience collective relief that we are not alone in our anxiety at being discovered.

My friend Bill, an entertaining psychologist, chided me with this insight: "That dream is caused by my psyche informing me that I am hiding issues I am afraid others will discover."

I don't know whether Bill's interpretation of my dream is accurate, but he may be right. I am comforted by the fact he told me he's had similar dreams. We can't escape reality—even in our sleep.

Recently I was counseling a mother and son about his poor school performance. As we began the discussion he blurted out, "Yes I have been taking drugs, but not very often." His mother and I were stunned. Drugs had not even been mentioned, but his opening up brought great relief to him. It's amazing how disclosing our wrongs brings about instant relief.

Real truth is correction's travel mate. Correction, without truth shared in love, is death disguised as wisdom. Whenever I've confessed an error and faced the truth, I always feel free, very free. Honesty is the necessary ingredient when we are wrestled down by the truth. And that is why this book is so important. The ability to give and receive criticism is a gift of great freedom.

Stop Running

Our fears keep us from facing reality. Fear keeps us from understanding God's mercy. A friend of mine articulated in a sermon, "A cry for mercy always gets God's ear." Fear is the enemy of the truth. Fear creates its own rules. Recognizing fear sets the stage for grace, but lies have many disguises. Lies disguise themselves in many ways. It's important to know the many disguises of fear that barricade our way to maturity. Some of the disguises of fear are:

- **Fear as wisdom.** The first sin in the garden was fear. Fear can sound like wisdom. The serpent counseled Eve about the fear of being insignificant: "God knows that if you eat the fruit you will be equal with him." The deceiver sounded wise beyond words. I have found people with poor motivation who will use criticism as a promise of success and safety, but, in reality, it brings discouragement. True wisdom is optimistic. True wisdom shows the way through an issue, not the way around it.
- **Fear as strength.** Sometimes because we fear we will look weak, we reject criticism. Our fear in those instances poses as strength. We say to ourselves, *Who do these people think they are? I'm strong and can stand alone without their input.* So we live deceived by our own fears while rejecting their rebuff. Many strong people have found, too late, that real strength comes from humility.
- **Fear as privilege.** Other times we demand the right to choose our critics. We shut down people we perceive to be inferior to us, because we see ourselves as all wise. We fear the loss of status if we admit wrong to a subordinate. But no one is too low to help us improve. True wisdom recognizes that no one can truly succeed without openness before all people.
- **Fear as safety.** The instinct to survive is powerful. If you've been raised in a verbally abusive home, any criticism can feel life threatening. If there's a choice between survival and destruction, you fight to survive. Wisdom and the need to survive get confused. As a result, you run from any discovery of your imperfection.

No one has ever died from being criticized, but I've had a few times in my life when I felt the criticism would overwhelm and bury me. Now I see my strong reactions against criticism were nothing more than my fear of being hurt.

Regaining Perspective

While waiting for an airplane in Dallas, Texas, my eye caught an interesting book title—*My Husband Is a Hat* by Oliver Sack. I stood and read several anecdotal stories of mentally ill people whom Dr. Sack had treated. One story tells of a woman who saw a hat every time she looked at her husband. Incredible! I know my wife sees many things when she looks at me, but she's never seen me as a hat.

I couldn't get that story out of my mind as I traveled back to Seattle. I began to wonder, *Are there people I view as hats?* I know I don't, but I did take inventory regarding my commitment to reality.

I wear glasses, but I don't enjoy wearing them. I lose three or four pair a year. My wife, Lori, keeps an extra pair around as a spare. I first realized I needed to wear glasses after twice walking off a speaking platform. I have a lazy eye and it crosses slightly affecting my depth perception. Anything around my right foot is in danger of being stepped on when I'm not wearing glasses.

Both times I walked off a speaker's platform, I appeared to be three or four feet from the edge of the stage. The first time I was preaching about how forgiveness was something we express to bring release to our own miserable hearts. I was emphasizing the miserable part, and all at once I was sitting in the lap of a very startled, middle-aged woman. I twisted my ankle, but she was fine. My pride was shattered for a few days.

The second time I fell off the platform I was telling a story about an unruly horse our family owned. I was imitating how the horse would try to step on our toes as we tried to saddle it. Suddenly I was on the floor laying in front of a laughing eight-year-old child. I had to accept the fact that my view wasn't consistent with reality. My eyes are bad. My friends and family convinced me after the second fall that I needed corrective glasses.

I still suffer with depth perception when I drive the car in reverse. I've backed into the same tree in my driveway at least ten times over a two-year period. Objects seem several feet away when I see them in my rearview mirror. I promised my wife after my last collision that I would back up only if I had someone helping me. I've learned to trust another's perception over my own when I back up. There are times in life when the criticism of others can help us avoid a major life collision. Often we need someone riding "shotgun" like the riders in the old stagecoach companies. The rider existed for one purpose—to watch the driver's blind spot for enemies.

God—Our Welcomed Critic

I've learned that self-criticism is the highest form of criticism. But our heart needs a critic who knows us and accepts us completely. I do a presentation on the Ten Commandments where I spell out these commands as the rules of greatness while addressing the spirit of relativism that denies any ultimate ethical authority. I point out that I want a judge who knows all there is to know, who always has my best interests in mind, and who understands me completely. I can't trust my own view of reality, but I can trust God as my ultimate and chosen critic.

God's criticism can be a friend because it's always consistent with who he is. Learning to hear his corrective input is made safe by knowing him personally. Are there ways we can be prepared to remember what God is like? I've found that by knowing the meanings of names attributed to God, I have a clearer understanding of who he is. These names reveal God's self-disclosure to us. Reviewing these names and traits of God show us that God is a healthy critic.

- *El Elyon*—God Most High
  This descriptive word means that God is the highest point of all there is. His vantage point is higher than ours. I trust his

confrontation because from his vantage point he sees all, and he is never caught in the web of this world's fate.

- *El Shaddai*—God Almighty
  Psalm 91:1, 2 invite us to live in the shadow of the Almighty. I need never fear self-discovery when I live under his shadow. All truth is healing truth when he covers me.

- *El Roi*—God Who Sees Me
  This description doesn't mean he is just watching to catch me doing wrong, but it means he loves me so much he can't take his eyes off of me.

- *Jehovah-Jireh*—God Will Provide
  I need not fear loss or scarcity. God, our judge, always has more than enough and will give to us abundantly. He is never lacking in resources to help in times of need.

- *Jehovah-Shalom*—God Is Our Peace
  God is not addicted to crises. He brings peace where it seems impossible. I have learned there is no more peaceful moment than when a correction is accepted.

- *Immanuel*—God With Us
  God puts on my shoes and runs alongside me. He is not ashamed to embrace me in my moments of repentance.

- *Jehovah-Rapha*—God Who Heals
  In Exodus 15 God promises to make whole any who might be broken by illness or tragedy. God's intention in all correction is to put the pieces back together for us. He is the God who takes broken Humpty-Dumpties and puts them together again.

The wonderful hope of Christlike criticism is that it never visits us alone; it always comes with two travel partners—grace and mercy. Reality is the by-product of correction, and reality is made tolerable by God's mercy and grace. As Christians we can embrace the pain of correction, because we know that rejection is not how God deals with openhearted people.

Reacting to Criticism

LET'S FACE IT: Criticism always draws out an array of emotions in any of us—some good, some not so good. That's just a fact of life, and we can't escape it. The good news, however, is that we can always choose to do something positive with criticism, and it can even make a significant contribution to our spiritual growth.

> He has a right to criticize who has a heart to help.
> ABRAHAM LINCOLN
>
> He who listens to a life giving rebuke will be at home with the wise.
> PROVERBS 15:33

In my history of speaking in nearly a dozen countries thus far, it seems I've had nearly every experience that Hollywood writers could create. By far, one of the most notable was the time I spoke at the wrong church in Poland.

I was running late in traveling from Warsaw to a little village in the central part of the country. It was the early 1980s, and quite an impressive youth movement was taking place in this little town, in

1

addition to the tension that was always present from one of the Warsaw Pact's regiments located in the community. A Lutheran church had asked me to conduct a series of evangelism meetings with their local rock band as the inspirational music.

I peeled into the main street of town and saw a Lutheran church on the left as soon as my wheels straightened out. I pulled up in front, grabbed my jacket, ran in the small, musty building, and told the pastor I was there and ready to speak.

He looked bemused but replied, "OK." The people sang a few songs, the women on one side and the men on the other. When the singing came to an end, the pastor looked at me, said a few words in Polish, and invited me to come up and speak.

I was having a great time teaching from Psalm 51. The people seemed quite interested, and even the pastor, though his face was frozen in a persistent look of perplexity, appeared captivated, smiling broadly with approval. This really encouraged me, and I was on a roll. The longer I spoke, the more I wondered why the rock band hadn't shown up.

I was moving into the last few verses of the psalm when three young people came through the sanctuary door and began motioning to me to follow them—even as I spoke. Not knowing if they were from the local community youth party, I decided it was safer to continue my sermon.

I was within five minutes of a glorious close when the three youths slipped up beside the pastor and whispered something into his ear. Then he stepped up and whispered something to the translator. The translator turned to me and said, "You need to finish up—you're in the wrong Lutheran church."

I soon discovered that nearly everyone there understood English despite the presence of the translator, because they all broke out in laughter. I waved good-bye and followed my new escorts. The folks at the correct church had been patiently waiting for me. This time I was allowed to finish my sermon uninterrupted.

This story reminds me that despite our best efforts, sometimes we end up in the wrong place doing the wrong things. And worse yet, they can *feel so right.* Several popular love songs ask the age-old question "How can it be wrong when it feels so right?" Easily. And in those difficult times when we find ourselves doing all the wrong things even when our motives might have been pure, we need to be open to correction.

Possible Reactions to Criticism

We may react in any number of ways when confronted with criticism. Think carefully—which of the following have characterized your reactions in the past couple of weeks?

- Denial
- Traumatic feelings of rejection
- Anger
- Attack
- Defensiveness
- Desire to change
- Thanks
- Prayer

Predicting your responses to criticism can be like trying to discern where land mines are hidden on a battlefield—extremely difficult, if not downright impossible. Our reactions to criticism reveal our inner state and cannot be managed without determined effort and skill. So it's imperative that we discover the negative responses we have to correction and replace them with thoughtful, Spirit-led reactions.

Typically our reactions to criticism come from emotional experiences in our developing years. The Christian's call is to live deliberately, not accidentally. This is a never-ending assignment, because we're always developing new negative reactions to correction. These work into the fiber of our personality and soon shape our response to any assessment.

A number of years ago I hosted a very well-known Christian figure for our congregation. He was a terrific communicator—and like many other creative people, he was highly sensitive to criticism.

As we were eating lunch together, he asked me what I thought of his message. I actually thought it was a little too long and that he hadn't followed the guidelines that I had laid out. However, the congregation seemed to enjoy it, so I told him that it was really good.

He asked again. "No, really—how did you think I did?"

So I told him. I explained that, frankly, it was too long, he hadn't followed my guidelines, and that was why he wasn't as effective as he could have been. His face turned red. I could tell that my observation that he hadn't been perfect traumatized him. So I added, "But other than that, you're the best speaker we've had outside myself!" My comment didn't help soothe his pain.

He went on to explain that he had never been good at receiving criticism. "I was put down and teased all my life," he said. "As a child I wasn't very athletic, and my brothers made fun of me because of that." To my surprise, his comments quickly became more positive as he opened up to me. He thanked me for telling him the truth but added that it was very difficult for him to hear and accept it.

He then paused and asked, "Do you think I'll ever get over it?" I jokingly replied, "No, I don't think so." I thought he was going to start crying, and I realized that I had genuinely hurt him. Putdowns, criticism, and the press to be perfect make it difficult for anyone; they obviously affect some people more profoundly than others. My friend still appeared to be wounded even after I apologized for my teasing. From that experience I've learned to be very careful with sensitive people.

I sometimes have trouble concentrating when I read and also have a mild form of dyslexia. I'm particularly prone to trouble writ-

REACTING TO CRITICISM 5

ing out numbers. Though I can do rapid-fire math calculations in my head, *writing* numbers causes me problems. Those who suffer from dyslexia, I'm told, experience life very differently from those who don't have this handicap. My difficulties in this area seem to be more pronounced at some times more than others. Especially under stress, I have a difficult time with numbers and spelling, particularly with words that sound alike.

My fourth grade teacher was a stickler on penmanship—and I just couldn't write under pressure. If she had just given me a bit more time, I could have done all right. Instead, she kept me after school day after day after day. I soon felt great despair about my writing abilities, and it seemed to get only slightly better after hours of work after school.

I lived with a great sense of humiliation and shame about the way I wrote. I recently got over it when I saw a piece of unedited writing by Bill Gates (founder of Microsoft). I learned to compensate and hide my problem, but it remained a struggle for years.

It was a breakthrough experience to be able to laugh about my writing. I have had a few adult friends, though, who didn't realize the level of difficulty I have with words, and they made fun of me. It truly hurt (until I realized that some of my writing really was hilarious). They particularly made fun of the way I confuse words that sound alike. I therefore became hypersensitive to any criticism about my writing or typing.

Similarly, I developed a poor response to anyone who said anything negative about my penmanship. A usual reaction of many people is to go on the attack by bringing up faults of the other person who first leveled the criticism. I hate to admit it, but that became my reaction to criticism or embarrassment.

I learned that the only way I could control my reactions was to understand where my critics came from. A friend told me that if I could accept the way God made me and did the best I could, who cared what anyone else thought? It made sense, so I decided my response would be just that from then on. Accepting yourself is the first step toward being open to learning from others.

Stopping Our Negative Reactions at the Source

Our families are the training grounds where we learn to embrace or run from criticism. I was the teaser in our family. I tormented my brother—and the truth about all tormentors is that we're bullies until converted. A tease can make another fear criticism and fight back at the slightest indication of disapproval. An often-overlooked fact is that it isn't just parents who impact us in our childhood.

I grew up with a fairly intense need to be perfect. My dad was competent in so many areas that I think it was hard for him to understand why some of us just couldn't keep up. Despite the fact that the relationships within my family were quite healthy, to this day I can't accept criticism without feeling I let everyone down. All of us who were raised by a perfectionist fight this for years. When families become perfectionists, their children experience a life filled with the fear of rejection, and it often manifests itself in recrimination.

Our school experience is another arena that programs our responses to life. We peer out at the world through windows that were shaped when we were small. The early years in school indelibly shape our views about life. If we grow up being called names in school, we freeze in confrontational situations. I was called "Red Skelton" in school, and I didn't like it. The pain of put-downs etches fear deeply into our hearts. But the good news is that we can put an end to the pain and fear that block our growth.

Sometimes a person just has to decide to stop the pain. I recall a friend of mine named Gordon who shared a class with me in the eighth grade. His nickname was "Porky." The name is self-explanatory. One day in a ninth grade physical education class Gordon had his fill with that nickname and blew up emotionally. He began swinging a jump rope at the whole class, and many of his swaths landed some pretty nasty blows. We never called him Porky again.

Our experience in our formative years can set us up for blow-ups like that. However, more often than not, we just bury the pain, ready to blow up if we feel threatened. Painful criticism that isn't healed can build up and cause us to explode in the face of even loving correction. If we can understand this, we're more likely to benefit from accountability to those around us.

Depression and Criticism

Some adolescent students appear to be sliding into the "bad kid" syndrome, but often the issue is poor self-esteem manifested through paralyzing self-criticism. For the most part, we all parent ourselves as we've been parented, and we're all friends to ourselves in the same manner others have treated us. Most troubled kids have had their self-esteem beaten down by someone, so they seek out friends who will accept them unconditionally. This is great, but more often than not, troubled kids find each other. And all learning stops at this juncture.

People with good self-esteem don't gravitate toward friends who make them feel inferior. I can't remember ever being taught how to chose a friend. Like most, I chose friends who were "easy." It would have done me a lot of good to find those who stretched and challenged me. I wish I had learned that friends can sometimes make you feel bad while doing you good.

Depression and other mood disorders cause self-esteem to drop. It elicits extreme reactions from their sufferers when they feel criticized. Low self-esteem is a wicked taskmaster. Depression-induced esteem loss can take a person so low that any criticism can seem like a fatal blow. It is vitally important for anyone experiencing depression to seek professional help.

Depressed people isolate themselves, making it difficult to help them. They often hide from others in ways that can be dangerous.

Depression can also have a component of paranoia. It's difficult to hear criticism if you feel the entire world is out to injure you. You can't grow emotionally if you fear everyone and every conflict.

Negative self-talk and self-loathing are both ingredients that make for a fearful reaction to criticism. If you feel you amount to little, you have no desire to hear anyone else confirming that thought. The soul is starved in the environment of self-deprecation, but it refuses to be fed. When the depressed person is the object of criticism, he or she either explodes or withers and then goes into a corner, so recriminating himself or herself that he or she can't take any more criticism from outside—the inner criticism is more than sufficient. Thus, rather than becoming a lifelong learner, the depressed person becomes a lifelong runner.

Some symptoms of depression to watch for:

Insomnia
Paranoia
Relational conflict
Agitation
Short-term memory loss
Weight loss or gain
Lowered self-esteem
Sleeping too much
Hostility
Blue moods
Loss of interest in hobbies or enjoyable activities
Loss of libido
Feelings of being overwhelmed
Isolation
Parents who are alcoholics or depressed
Difficulty focusing
Retarded learning ability

Depression is a chief enemy to growth. It makes every critic seem like an assassin. If your reactions are excessive when you're criticized, you may create an assassin—and you may also be struggling with traces of depression.

Depressed persons typically choose friends who are destructive to them or spouses who remind them of their weaknesses. These friends or spouses often press them toward the sense of rejection they have grown accustomed to.

Do you see any possibility that medical or inner emotional issues might be dictating your life rather than God's wisdom? What might be some of the sources of your reactions to criticism? Are there any that come from your family that you need to quell? Or do you recognize symptoms of depression that indicate depression itself could be blocking your path to becoming a successful person?

Our Craving for Acceptance

Acceptance is the greatest gift a family can give a child. While positive criticism is valuable, we also need people in our lives who make us feel accepted, wanted, and especially *needed*. The ability to resist feelings of rejection is one of the key ingredients in living a successful life. Growing people have their friendships in balance. We need people who correct us, but just as important, we need to be accepted even in our failing moments. Success is never a solo effort—it requires partners. It requires loving critics who accept us.

Total and complete honesty is the best gift a school can offer children in their early years. And honest acceptance of what we're good at and what we're not good at is essential to human growth. The ability to face assessment allows us to embrace and grow all our lives, becoming lifelong learners. However, it takes work and vigilance to embrace the process. Indeed, there is no learning without criticism.

I love to oil paint. There are a few people who even like my paintings. It took me a long time before I would show anyone anything I painted. The first time I took a painting to our offices and hung it in a prominent place in my office, one of my youth workers came into my office and noticed that my initials were painted in the lower right corner.

"Did you paint that, boss?" he asked.

I wanted to say no. I was so afraid he would laugh. And that's exactly what he did when I said, "Yes." I was crushed. I acted as if I thought it was funny, too, but I decided right then and there that I had better hide my artistic endeavors.

I didn't paint anything else for weeks. I had decided that if I couldn't be any good at it, I wouldn't paint at all. I had enough criticism as a pastor without creating another opportunity to be put down. A few others on our team noticed I had created the painting. I received some compliments, but most of the viewers just looked in silence. A few days later I took the painting down.

Any artistic venture is very stressful. The reason? You put part of yourself into it. It's hard to objectify yourself in art.

I kept forgetting to take the painting home. It sat for weeks in the corner of my assistant's office. One afternoon some of our creative arts team were working on my assistant's office, and one of them, a professional artist, saw my "masterpiece" in the corner.

"I really like that painting," she said. "It's unique."

I didn't say a word, standing still and acting as though I hadn't heard her. Then my assistant spoke up.

"Doug painted it. I like it, too, but he won't let us hang it up."

The artist asked if she could have it to hang with a collection she was showing. I said no at first—but she eventually walked out with the thing, and I've never seen it since.

Because of this incident, I did start painting again. I was actually filled with intense creativity when I got home to my studio that night.

Later I asked the artist if she saw anything I could improve in my paintings. She thought for a moment and said, "Well, the composition structure could have been lined up better with a center reference." She went on to teach me how to improve my brush strokes and to mix my paints so that the colors were consistent.

I soared with confidence from her instruction. Why? She first identified where my talents could take me and then was a good enough friend to give me helpful criticism.

Lifelong Learners and Criticism

Some of the consistent traits of lifelong learners are found in Psalm 37. Here David tells us not to fret over evildoers. The word here is to not be in terror of the experiences you have with those who tear you down. Instead, look for God's affirmation. He says that if you delight yourself in him, he will give you the desires of your heart. And he went on to say that if you commit your way to him, he would be worthy of that commitment.

Fear-based responses to life keep us from learning. In fact, fear really keeps us immature at all ages. Outbursts of anger in the face of assessment are a sure sign that we're living a fear-based life.

The following are some of the important traits that lifelong learners develop:

- **God esteem.** This is different from self-esteem. The person with God esteem believes what God says about him or her.
- **Open hearts.** A person who is open to sharing his or her life with others, meeting new friends, and facing new challenges spends his or her life seeing the IQ for success grow.
- **A failure-friendly attitude.** Lifelong learners have found that finding who they *are* is the pathway to self-discovery. And they also know every failure is a further assurance that success is on the way.
- **Natural curiosity.** Secure people are usually curious. If you aren't hiding and are always finding new things in life, you'll find yourself on the president's list of any school.
- **Gratefulness.** Lifelong learners find a reason to be thankful for everything they have and experience.
- **Self-containment.** Self-contained people live from the inside out. Blows that come from the outside in just don't have the impact that inside-out beliefs do.

- **Honest appraisal of themselves.** Lifelong learners embrace criticism, because they've learned they can't be good at everything. They accept their incompetence. And from there they build on their strengths.
- **Belief that God is their Defender.** It's a relief when you no longer have to protect yourself from the world. Successful people like David have learned that with God on your side there's absolutely nothing to fear.

Your Life Metaphors

Did you know you could change the metaphors that drive your life? Do you realize that metaphors could be affecting your personal growth and your ability to learn? A metaphor is a symbol of reality. It helps us define our world.

Have you ever said, "I feel like a slob today"? I have. I'm really not a slob, but the term fits me occasionally. I call my wife (who's from Germany), my "German girl" when she behaves in that serious, stern way typical of many Germans. It's fun to use metaphors.

If you can tell me your metaphors for life, I can tell you how anxious you are, how easily you take criticism, and whether you're learning much. Consider the following list of metaphorical and other types of statements that might be controlling you.

- My life is a test.
- My life is a terror.
- My life is a wonderful journey.
- My life is a learning experience.
- My life will have an end.
- My life is filled with acceptance.
- My life is filled with discoveries.
- Life is a journey with others.
- My life is forever improving.

Attitudes That Become Enemies

Our attitudes make us who we are. Some attitudes are healthy, while others become enemies to God's work in our lives. Learning to hear a loving correction requires work on the attitudes that occupy our minds.

Your attitudes toward others can make the difference between a life of joy and a life of loneliness and underachievement. Are you frozen by a need to be perfect? Do you find that your attitude toward others brings out the worst in them when they seek to help you?

Take a moment and begin your contemplation with the following list:

I'm not good enough.
I must be perfect.
I'll be rejected.
If they really knew me they would hate me.

Think about these four statements, and you'll soon discover that you can see criticism as a friend. And you'll be a valuable member of any group you're in. You'll find yourself becoming "the real you."

"I'm Not Good Enough"

Let's take on the first deadly life descriptive phrase "I'm not good enough." There are plenty of times when we're not up to the task that life presents us. But with God's power in us, we'll always be able to stand up, because he will never allow us to be tempted beyond our ability to withstand.

The recurrence in the Gospels of the story of the feeding of the five thousand with just a small amount of bread and fish is a great reminder to us that *whatever we have plus God always gets the job done.* So you may not be strong enough, good enough, or smart enough, but what you have with God will always be sufficient to face life. Therefore, you can learn from life and enjoy it.

"I Must Be Perfect"

"I must be perfect" is a torturous enemy. Healthy thinking allows us to be ourselves. No one is ever perfect. I have rejected the notion that when the church world gets perfect, God will finally act—if for no other reason than that it's impossible to believe that sufficient numbers of Adam's race will get pure enough to make God's work contingent upon our works. Grace is the only pathway into God's work.

God chose to act on the day of Pentecost. We survive and thrive in Christ's perfection—not our own. In fact, we'll never be perfect in this life in the sense of acting and thinking perfectly at all times. But 1 John reminds us that we have an Advocate before the Father.

"I'll Be Rejected"

All humans fear rejection. All fear not fitting in. Replace these thoughts of rejection with the acknowledgment that God accepted you and the Bible's instruction that we're to accept one another. The interesting thing about acceptance and rejection is you usually receive what you give out to others. The practice of loving and accepting others will lead to self-acceptance and love. The truth is that whenever you're rejected, you can count on there being another situation in which you'll be accepted.

Could it be that even rejection is a gift from God? Could rejection be intended to force us to find the place of true affirmation in God himself?

"If They Really Knew Me They Would Hate Me"

Many people have free-floating guilt—they've never learned to genuinely embrace forgiveness. They fail to see that their sins are completely cast away from them by receiving Christ's forgiveness. Sometimes this can be due to not letting go and turning away from life's failings and admitting that they'll always fall hopelessly short of being fully good. It could be that there are some errors in their lives that cause them to fear rejection across the board. Experiencing forgiveness is a great step toward being able to receive input into our lives.

King David said that as long as he tried to hide his sin and errors, his bones began to decay and he withdrew into isolation, but when he came out into the open, he realized that God heard and healed him (see Ps. 32:3, 4).

All of us struggle and have occasional errors in our lives. Remember—if you believe that you're the only one as bad as you are, you've been lied to. God wants to free you from your sin and your guilt and is ready to do so as soon as you ask him to.

The Purpose of Criticism

WHY IS CRITICISM such a big part of life? Is it really necessary? Why won't it just go away?

I asked a group of pastors once if they liked an idea I had for dealing with criticism. What if we could pick two years in our lives when we would be criticized from morning to night— and then the rest of our lives people would just leave us alone? Wouldn't that be great?

Criticism has a purpose beyond tempering our pride. If

> Be careful and self-defacing when you correct people who are wrong. Maybe then you will lead them to turn to him and accept the truth.
>
> 2 TIMOTHY 2:25, 26
> (Author's paraphrase)

> Everything in the Scriptures is God's Word—all of it is designed for learning, nudging and correcting people to live the right way.
>
> 2 TIMOTHY 3:16
> (Author's paraphrase)

> You must correct people and point out their sins. But also help them see how happily they can improve when you instruct them, and always let the response be in God's hands.
>
> 2 TIMOTHY 3:4
> (Author's paraphrase)

we believe in the biblical description of God, we have to believe he intends criticism for grand purposes.

If we can understand why we face criticism, I think it will be easier to make it work for us.

The first reason criticism is such a part of life is that we all get off course. And none of us has the ability to stay on course without help. As Isaiah said, "We all, like sheep, have gone astray, each of us has turned to his own way" (Isa. 53:6). And as soon as we become Christians, we're in the process of "becoming." The journey to the "real us" requires some serious guidance—and "becomers" can be dangerous when left to themselves.

Imperfect people are the only ones who need correction—and that's every one of us. Since the fall of humanity, evaluation has been necessary. Today's culture is committed to a not-so-benign relativism, which is an attempt to create a world without correction. And so far the experimentation with relativism is failing miserably. Why? We're all so imperfect that serious measures are required to keep us on course.

Criticism is necessary to keep us healthy. Even in the case of a very serious disease, the last to know is often the sufferer. Our soul diseases affect us like the proverbial frog in the boiling kettle.

I attended a conference a few years ago that focused on effective public speaking. The array of speakers for the event was quite impressive. However, the keynote speaker had forgotten to zip his trousers. I knew everyone could see his situation that morning—it was quite obvious. But no one even during the break risked pointing out the problem to him. The poor man went through three sessions on display. Just as it was getting almost unbearably uncomfortable, he asked, "How many of you noticed my pants were unzipped?"

We all raised our hands. And we all felt pretty stupid, because we could tell by the tone of his voice that he had done this deliberately.

"You can't be a good communicator unless you're willing to learn confronting love," he said. "Good communication means being able to tell your audience that their fly's down."

It was a great lesson to all of us. We saw that not confronting a friend can actually result in more embarrassment than what results from criticizing them. Let's take some time to consider several reasons to refrain from criticizing.

1. Criticism Should Not Be Used to Ventilate

I was in a grocery store the other day near my home when I saw a man shopping with all three of his children in tow. He was clearly not enjoying the experience. He had his hands full corralling one darling little girl of about ten years of age and two handsome little guys, one about eight years old and the other about six. They followed him with gleeful defiance with a clear determination to put Dad to the test.

As I sauntered behind them, I could feel the tension rising. The father was clearing his throat more loudly with each frustrated step. I decided to leave him with his struggles and hurried through my list of items.

I went through my checkout counter at the same time as this little horde. As I strolled by them with a smile, I heard one of the kids ask his dad if he knew where the car was. The kids laughed and pointed to the car next to mine. Then the oldest boy to whom the hapless dad had given the keys wouldn't give them back. A squabble ensued. I took my time loading my car, sensing something entertaining was about to happen.

Finally with the keys handed over, the man opened the sliding door of their Astro van. Then the daughter grabbed a bag from the top just exactly the way her father had asked her not to do. The father screamed out, "There you go again, stupid! Don't you ever do anything right? I don't think I can ever have you go to the grocery store with me again if you're going to be so irresponsible!" [I've cleaned up his speech a little bit for the purposes of this book.]

He had ventilated. He had criticized his daughter. Actually, he had humiliated her. The children were frozen with fear. Getting the steam out of our lives is a necessary part of being healthy, but it's risky to others when we use them as our targets.

Ventilating is always followed by remorse. As I climbed into my truck right next to his, I heard the father begin to apologize. He said he was just getting "frustrated." Sometimes we have rough days, and we start looking for people to criticize and relieve some of the steam. This kind of criticism is always destructive.

I doubt that any of us have missed the opportunity to be the target for another's ventilation. And sadly enough, all of us have likely blown off a little steam at the expense of others. I always feel terrible when I do. Criticism was never designed by God to be a safety valve for frustrating days.

2. Criticism Should Not Be Used to Change Other People

There is only one person qualified to change the world—God. And he's the only one who can genuinely change you and me. Many parents buy into the myth that they can control their kids. No one I have seen has ever really controlled the ones under their charge. We may pretend to be under submission, but we always find ways to make it known that we will be what we want. One way or another, whether it's passively, aggressively, or covertly, we all resist having others seek to dismantle and put us back together.

Many a well-meaning spouse has made his or her main project in life changing the person he or she married. Our efforts to make someone into our likeness always fail. And even if domestic engineers get what they want, they usually don't like it—because it's a twin staring them back in the face.

Criticism is a gift of love to another. We're called to speak the truth, and God does the changing. *All changing should be left in the hands of God.* Genuinely good criticism is a gift of vital information that will help another change. The emphasis should be on *help.*

I wish I had fifty cents for every time I've heard a spouse say, "I've lived with this man [woman] for twenty years, and I still can't get him [her] to change." My thoughts have always been, *Well, thank God. Wouldn't it be terrible if the whole world were made in our image?*

I knew of a family who didn't like their son's choice of a wife. They tried everything to get her to change. They criticized her for the way she dressed, the way she cooked, and the way she spoke. They couldn't let a day go by without belittling the love of their son's life.

They also began to criticize their son, saying he was irresponsible. He was actually the most responsible young man I've ever met. They began to criticize him for his grades. His grades went up, so then they began attacking his career choice. It seemed they felt they could separate the two by the persistence of their criticism. The tragic part of the story is that his parents were ministers.

The couple came in tears to see me. The young lady said, "What can I do? I'm in an environment where I'll not be accepted or received. They criticize me constantly. They want me to change before they'll allow their son to love me."

My response was simple: "There's only one person in all the universe you're supposed to change for, and that's God. So ignore their criticisms while maintaining an attitude of respect. It's possible they just may have something to point out that might help you improve. If they do give you some good advice, thank them." I really believe that responding to disrespect with respect up to a point can genuinely heal a situation loaded with fear.

3. Criticism Should Not Be Used to Put Someone in His or Her Place

Whenever criticism is used to put someone in his or her place, it brings only death. Some toxic critics love to point out errors of others in order to make it clear that they're superior. We've all been witnesses to this pattern.

Sometimes people with low self-esteem get a lift from criticizing others. There is a good sensation that can be felt for a moment by pointing out how wrong everyone around us is. The worse we can make others look, the more easily we can feel that we just might be OK after all. Low self-esteem is a culprit in all toxic criticism. If you don't feel good about yourself, why not enjoy another's stupidity?

Criticism given to put us down must be rejected. We can't be passive about the abusive behavior of our critics. I know I'll never accept criticism from someone who clearly wants to use me to get a self-esteem lift at my expense.

4. Loving Criticism Never Intends to Hurt

Many of us know someone we would love to punish. Criticism intended to punish another is always poisonous. Paul wrote in Galatians 6:2, "Carry each other's burdens." In the previous verse he wrote, "If someone is caught in a sin, you who are spiritual should restore him gently." This is a far different approach than going on the attack. Trying to "punish" someone into line is far from carrying his or her burdens.

I've sat in on many meetings in church in which staff people or laypeople were raked over the coals. The intent of these meetings, sometimes, is to make the person feel punished. Far too many Christian leaders believe guilt, fear of punishment, and beating someone down are the right ways to motivate.

Here's a little test to see if you're sliding into toxic criticism yourself. If you ever want to criticize and there's any delight in your heart that the person is finally "getting theirs," you have a serious problem. It would be best for everyone if you just kept your mouth shut.

Punishment has no place in criticism. The truth is that we all punish ourselves more than enough. There's no need for criticism to be painful. It may indeed be painful, but a good correction may just bring jubilation and joy, and it could also give the recipient courage. Isn't it wonderful when joy replaces fear?

5. Criticism Has No Part in Competition

Leading by intimidation is the predilection of many leaders. I've often fallen into this mode, thinking things would work faster if I kept people in their place. Criticism can be a toxic tool to keep things on track until your ideas win. Life by intimidation is a killer. Many people have trouble with people they can't control. And they use their criticism to set boundaries and to limit those whom they lead.

Competition drives many critics in the office and home. I have had hundreds of people under my employment and have seen again and again how some, to advance in their careers, use criticism. There are a few instances I can remember easily.

One of our management people named Tim wanted in the worst way to move into ministry work. He had an accounting degree, and his management skills were great—but his "people" skills were in considerable need of development.

Tim had one particular pastor he decided needed to be set aside so he could get his chance, so he made an appointment to meet with our assistant in charge of personnel.

"I have a list here of ten major letdowns in Gordy's area," he said. "Would you like to go over them? My assistant told me that Tim sat quietly and seemed pleased with his list of Gordy's infractions.

My assistant calmly replied, "Tim, ministry around here isn't about competition—it's about partnership and teamwork. We really aren't interested in your ability to catch people at wrong. I'll go over this with Doug and the personnel team, but this isn't going to get you what you think."

Tim continued being a critic to those whom he felt were doing his job. It was really a sad ending, because Tim ended up being terminated. Criticism and competition are a bad mix if you want a life worth living.

There's no win-lose in the community of Jesus. We're to do the best that we can to bring out win-win outcomes. Godly criticism is never intended to help me get a higher score than you. It is instead intended to help us both discover how our journey can better honor Christ.

> Open rebuke is better than secret love. Faithful are the wounds of a friend; but the kisses of an enemy are deceitful.
> PROVERBS 27:5, 6, KJV

So why criticize? It's time to take note of the positive purpose of criticism. Hopefully all of us can become experts in the area of loving correction. It's a worthy aim. The following explains what our mentality should be when we admonish friends.

1. Criticism Is Instruction

Criticism is first of all instruction, teaching us how to live life. Sometimes Bible words allow us to paint pictures to help us understand fully the basic principles of life. I like to think of words as different shapes of an oil painting. Like brushes, they help us dabble with different visions on our life canvases.

One of the more creative words for "correction" is the Greek word *diorthōma*. This compound word was used to describe friendship at work helping a person reform. It also had courtroom applications for adding a legal amendment to a contract or correcting a mistake in a contract. Breaking the word down, we find the prefix *dia* (through) and the root word *orthos* (straight) coming together to mean "an instruction by way of correction." Interesting enough, the word also was used to describe "becoming."

So if a critic is a friend bringing loving correction, good could come from it. He or she has become your teacher. Only these teachers are helping you "become" the person you most want to be.

However, there are few things worse than an unwanted instructor. I have two friends I used to golf with regularly. If you've never golfed, don't start. If you play golf, you'll understand my story in full.

One of my golfing friends, Steve, has never played a round below ninety-two (that's not very good), yet you would think he was a teaching pro. When a group of us would golf with him, he could hold his tongue for about four holes, and then the instructions cascaded upon us. He would always start with instructing us on how to put the ball onto the tee, expounding his belief that it should be a little farther up off the ground than most players are comfortable with. Though some people disagree with him at first, they watch in wonder as he hits the ball off the tee and nearly lands it on the moon. The heightened tee position is set up to hit the ball off the planet.

Then there's Bill. Bill has one club he uses all the time—he calls it "Big Mama." It looks like a street lamp that someone took off and glued to a stick. He uses it for any range of shots, whipping it out of his bag anytime he's more than 80 yards from the pin. Sometimes he even putts with Big Mama, believing it has a mystic "vibe" that assures a good shot.

Many is the time that Bill has worn out the rest of his foursome with instructions on our hip movement. He knows exactly how to get the snap to your hips and then maintain good follow-through. Of course, we would all like to look more professional with our swings, but we're skeptical about Bill—because he looks utterly ridiculous when he swings. And I really get tired of being corrected by a teacher I didn't invite into my game. Uninvited teachers are hard to tolerate, especially when they aren't any better than we are.

Another good picture for learning is what musicians call "jamming." Sometimes I really wish I had become a professional record producer. I love to play guitar. My problem is that I never really mastered it. I can write a decent song and have been known to sing all right. In fact, I sing for a lot of my outreach events—but I'm definitely not a pro.

I love jamming with pros. One of my friends named Caleb is one of the world's best guitar players. In fact, Eric Clapton on "The David Letterman Show" said that Caleb was the best guitarist in the world. He has helped me with studio recordings, services, and some traveling evangelism.

The great part about playing with a pro in a jam session is that you learn by watching him or her play. And you'll hardly ever hear a pro say to you, "You sound terrible." More than likely, he or she will look over and say, "Have you ever thought of this . . . ?" It's such a wonderful thing to hear a pro say that instead of "Oh, wow—get me out of here!"

The better the pro, the more prone he or she is to be gracious, understanding, and helpful to someone on a lower achievement level. The effects of a poor player are just the opposite. We'll get to that topic later.

A jam is designed to help everyone polish his or her "chops," building around a simple theme, and allowing every player to take turns improvising off the theme. There's no judgment in a jam session—everyone gets the chance to try new licks and become a better player.

I think a jam session is a great picture of how godly criticism should work. Christians are supposed to be the real pros who are constantly encouraging even when the music is out of tune.

Correction in living relationships is like jamming. This careful interaction from friend to friend makes great music from life. Remember this metaphor next time you decide to give some advice. Will your advice make a song, or will it harm a team?

Another word for "correction" is the Greek word *epanorthōsis*, which is related to the other Greek word mentioned previously. The essential meaning is to restore to an upright state again. Correction from this word's viewpoint is pushing someone up straight again after he or she has fallen down. This is a fantastic picture.

In my college years I often helped my uncles in a family-owned construction business. My dad had long since left the business, but my two uncles had plenty of work for me during breaks. It was always wonderful work after spending weeks in a library.

I had the job one spring break of working with three other friends lifting prefabricated walls. We would lift the walls up a few feet horizontally and then place cinder blocks under them. The walls sat flat, solidly secured on the blocks about a foot off the floor. Then our job was to grab the ends, lift the walls off the blocks, and gently turn them up straight.

One of us had to tie a rope to the wall and hold back so the wall didn't fall back before it could be anchored into its straight-up position. Once the wall fell all the way back over onto the concrete floor. No one was too excited about the look of a wall that had slapped down onto a concrete floor with small pebbles on it.

Sometimes lifting another's "life walls" up straight is heavy work. This kind of helping is delicate work and takes great care. When we do this, we're being the best kind of teachers.

Another Greek word for criticism is *paideutēs*. It was one of the first words used for "instructor" and "corrector" and the one Paul used in Romans 2:20 to describe the role of the Law. This passage shows the Law as an instructor, or teacher, to prepare us for grace. Sometimes we become teachers with our criticism. And when we do, we prepare our friends for more grace.

Correction becomes a breath of fresh air when it's an act of love. You can't say you really love someone if you let him or her go on with life-destroying habits. Indifference is a long way from being loving.

I tend to have a stiff attitude at times. I've been called a borderline nerd. For some reason, dressing in a coordinated manner is not something I catch on to easily.

My daughter used to check me out regularly to see what I was wearing when I went out the door. Sure enough, I would often have two different shoes on or socks that don't match. She would say, "Dad, you can't go out that way—you'll embarrass us all!"

> He who ignores discipline despises himself, but whoever heeds correction gains understanding. The fear of the Lord teaches a man wisdom, and humility comes before honor.
> **PROVERBS 15:32, 33**
>
> Endure hardship as discipline; God is treating you as sons. For what son is not disciplined by his father?
> **HEBREWS 12:7**
>
> If you are not disciplined (and everyone undergoes discipline), then you are illegitimate children and not true sons.
> **HEBREWS 12:8**

I used to take it with a grain of salt—until one time I wore a pair of jeans that had a hole worn in the seat. I was running short on time and was headed out the door when she hollered down the stairs to me, "Dad, I haven't checked you out yet!"

I said, "I've got to go—I'm in a hurry!" I went on out to my engagement, which involved speaking to a crowd of approximately three thousand. Needless to say, I was embarrassed at that meeting when one of my friends pointed out that he could see the color of boxer shorts I was wearing that day. From that day forward, I learned the great value of my daughter's correction.

2. Criticism Causes Growth

I had two wonderful grandmas growing up. One was an incredible cook; the other was a big outdoors person. Grandma Murren was the one I spent the most time with. She felt it her primary obligation in life to make sure that her grandchildren grew up right.

> All scripture is given by inspiration of God, and is profitable for doctrine, for reproof, for correction, for instruction in righteousness: That the man of God may be perfect, thoroughly furnished unto all good works.
> 2 TIMOTHY 3:16, 17, KJV

She had an artistic way of helping guide her grandchildren and believed it was very important that we knew how to work. I well remember at thirteen years of age climbing cherry trees with Grandma in central Washington in 104-degree July weather. If you grow up in farm country, you learn quickly that work is a good thing.

She corrected us if we hung out at the water jug too long. If we sat down in the shade, she corrected us by working faster herself. Who can sit in the shade when his or her sixty-five-year-old grandmother is lugging around fruit? She would move her ladder around into the sun where she thought we should do it and would then climb up and begin working, saying, "This is how it's done."

She also wanted to make sure we ate right. For some reason, she got it in her mind that none of us grandkids were getting fed properly at home. She often said she didn't want to have any grandchildren looking skinny.

As a pastor, I've realized that the more I act like my grandmother, the more people seek my help. And the more I act unlike my grandmother, the less helpful I am. Modeling is the best way to teach. But it also requires verbal prodding to help people grow.

Climbing up into the tree with your own bucket in hand, clawing the cherries, and encouraging others on is a great image of what this is all about. If our aim is to help another grow with joy, then we're more likely to hit the mark. And the most effective critics are those who get right up into the trees with those they're working to help.

3. Criticism Restores

The New Testament word for "restore" is another picturesque one. The original word came from the fishing industry and meant "to mend the nets." Occasionally a fisherman's net would tear when it was scraped along a lakebed. Helpful correction is like mending one another's nets. It helps catch the most from life after it fixes us up.

> Brothers, if someone is caught in a sin, you who are spiritual should restore him gently. But watch yourself, or you also may be tempted. Carry each other's burdens, and in this way you will fulfill the law of Christ. If anyone thinks he is something when he is nothing, he deceives himself. Each one should test his own actions. Then he can take pride in himself, without comparing himself to somebody else, for each one should carry his own load.
> GALATIANS 6:1–5

Paul warned the Galatians that they were beginning to be too heavy-handed on fallen friends. Paul called the church to restore, not just to point out the wrong. The art of making a community requires speaking the truth. Yet according to Paul, it also requires gentleness and empathy.

Paul knew injured people are like wounded dogs—you must handle them with great care. Once on a rainy Seattle night, I was driving behind a station wagon that hit a large collie dog. The driver went on swiftly, ignoring the animal's cries. I pulled over to see just how badly the dog had been injured. It broke my heart to see the beautiful animal writhing in pain. I hoped it would have a chance to live, but I knew I had to get it off to the side of the road if he was to have a chance.

I cautiously put my hand under the dog's shoulders, hoping to gently slide him off to the side of the road. As I approached with a blanket, he lunged at me, growling and squealing. My first reaction was to think, *Well, fine—lie there and die, and see if I care!* But I moved on toward him and began to fit the blanket on the ground. Then with stunning force he turned and bit my arm.

His bite hurt—and bad! This made me angry. I mean, after all, I was only trying to help the poor animal. Why did he want to chew my arm off? Then it struck me—if I had just been hit by a truck and a collie dog came along and grabbed me and began pulling me off to the side of the road, I would act pretty dangerous too. I found the courage to wrap a coat around my arm and slide him off the road. A friend traveling with me took my car and sought help at a veterinary hospital. I visited the collie at the vet's several days later, and he was much friendlier. He lived—and it made the bruises on my arm seem like a trophy.

I've reacted to criticism just as the collie did to me on the side of the road. None of us take correction well when we're in pain. Even though we bark and bite, we really do appreciate the criticism later.

I recently helped transition a church through some difficult times. One of the leaders of the church said, "Well, we would have been able to keep our pastor, except that his attitude just got so sideways."

Having had my attitudes get sideways at times with God's folks, I had a great deal of empathy for the pastor. So I piped up and told them the story about the collie.

I concluded, "You simply had a pastor you beat up badly enough that he felt like a truck ran over him, and he started nipping." Why are we surprised that people needing to be healed get a little cranky about it? Correction is designed to take "becomers" who have holes torn in their life nets and help them back to health.

Our culture is growing more and more into a "face-saving" culture. Face-saving cultures rely on indirect communication to make points. The direct truth is sugar-coated. We're all becoming one large dysfunctional alcoholic family. We see the white elephant sitting in the corner of the room, no matter what it might be— someone who is angry, is an alcoholic, or is a disgruntled board member. Few have the courage to say, "Hey—we've got a problem that needs to be corrected. The community needs to be restored. The malfunctioning of the family needs someone to confront them. The backbiting and mean-spirited behavior has

> Against an elder receive not an accusation, but before two or three witnesses. Them that sin rebuke before all, that others also may fear.
> 1 TIMOTHY 5:19, 20

to go. Let's face the facts." I believe this is Paul's point in saying, "Restore them gently. Face the facts. But remember, broken people must be handled with care."

4. Correction Builds Community

God hates fear. It was the greatest enemy Israel faced in the Old Testament. And Jesus said again and again that we're to "fear not." Building communities that heal requires a fearless culture. After all, fear stops us from hearing criticism.

Paul said, "If you've got an elder who is talking the talk but doesn't walk the walk, you give him a chance to mend his ways. If he doesn't, take two or three witnesses, and then if he still won't repent, admonish him publicly." This public criticism was to be a warning to the whole church to stay on track.

That we should rebuke those who sin is a strong directive. "Sin" is truly a difficult word to use today, but it's one that we can't neglect. It means a lifestyle of consistently missing God's mark. Our aim is to stop it in its tracks.

I was walking through the airport in Chicago recently when I observed a family with six boys. Yes, six very frisky boys were frolicking through the airport with their bemused parents. The boys appeared to range in age from around six to around thirteen. One of the middle children kept trying to get ahead of the group. I concluded that he did this so he could get a candy bar without being noticed.

How did I know this? I overheard him ask his mother for a dollar bill. She stalled for a moment. Then he began reminding her that she owed him four dollars. Overhearing the exchange, Dad said, "You're not getting any sugar before the plane ride." Mom said, "That's right. You can have the dollar—but no candy."

The family soon found its way to the same gate as me. And they soon forgot the dollar and the young boy hungry for chocolate. It was a movie in the making. The son disappeared from view, claiming to need the rest room. Finally, a few moments later, he slipped back around a corner—with the last bite of a Snickers bar behind his back. The father yanked him by the back of the shirt and made him sit right beside him. That's a rebuke. A loving rebuke is intended to stop us right in our tracks.

Around 1959 my brother Todd and I were helping my grandfather repair the roof on my uncle's home. I was eight or nine, and my brother was five or six. Our grandfather was throwing the old roofing materials off the roof while Todd and I stacked it in a pile where they could be burned. Then, once the roof was cleared off, my granddad and my uncle began nailing down the new wood shingles.

It was nearly four in the afternoon, in the most oppressive heat of the summer day. My granddad accidentally dropped three new shingles, and they fell to the ground closest to Todd. I was about 15 feet away. Once they landed, my granddad yelled out to my brother, "Todd, would you please pick up those shingles and bring them up the ladder to me?"

It was at that moment that time seemed to stand still. All life went into slow motion. I could see the look on my brother's face—a look of defiance. Four in the afternoon on any July day in central Washington is not the time to fool with a man on a roof. But my brother was about to do it.

Looking up from where he was twirling dirt around with a stick, he said, "Get it yourself, old man!"

I couldn't breathe. I wanted to run. I wanted to say, "No, Todd! No, Todd! No, Todd!" But before I could even get another breath into my lungs, my granddad was a blur swooping down that ladder, heading toward Todd like a bull with nostrils flared. And as I expected, once he grabbed those shingles, he proceeded to spank my brother harder than I've ever seen anyone spanked.

I decided right then and there that anytime my granddad wanted something I would give it to him. My grandfather was by nature a loving, kind, gentle man—but he would not take defiance from any of his grandchildren. My brother was corrected, and I learned.

The sad thing is that some of us grown-ups become object lessons to others, even in a community of faith. This is different than being punished. Being stopped in your tracks so you don't destroy yourself in life is a good thing. And when others see you face this kind of confrontation, it's beneficial for us all.

Isn't deterrence part of the wisdom behind the sentences handed down to convicted criminals? I mean, what if your neighbor Harry down the road backed up a truck, loaded up twenty television sets from the local

> Comfort one another with these words.
> **1 THESSALONIANS 4:18, KJV**
>
> Encourage one another daily, as long as it is called Today; so that none of you may be hardened by sin's deceitfulness. We have come to share in Christ if we hold firmly till the end the confidence we had at first.
> **HEBREWS 3:13, 14**
>
> He who ignores discipline comes to poverty and shame, but whoever heeds correction is honored.
> **PROVERBS 13:18**

Circuit City, and then when he went to court the judge said, "We'll give you a couple weeks down in Key West so you can think about this"?

Now how many others would begin thinking, *Hey—I think I'll go clean out a store, too. I can use a week's rest in Key West.* No, what we hear about is that our neighbor Harry had to spend $30,000 on an attorney and then six months in the county jail plus three years on probation. His life is ruined. We all learn from this episode in neighbor Harry's life not to even think of trying to do what he did. So correction is intended, in a loving way, to let the community know there are consequences to your actions.

5. Correction Brings Courage

Some words are hard to define by simply using other words. One of these is "encourage," a simple three-syllable word built out of the prefix "en," meaning "in," and the word "courage," meaning "boldness to face life."

I thoroughly loved the movie *Braveheart*, which starred Mel Gibson. The depiction of William Wallace was so inspiring that I went and grabbed my drawing pencils and oils so I could make a painting of this great Scottish warrior.

For years the higher lords of the Scottish tribes had been appeasing the British with taxes and overpayments. None of them liked it, but none of them would risk their own status with the British to attack them.

Then along came Wallace, leader of the rabble and the common men against the British. Just the presence of Wallace raised the courage of the other lords to challenge the British. This in itself is correction.

One of the unfortunate aspects of my being a pastor is that people often believe that I can see down into the tiptoes of their heart and diagnose their sins. Truth is, that's not been one of the

Lord's gifts to me. And also I've never cared much for picking around in other people's faults.

But something about the office of a pastor in and of itself has a sort of correction to it. The key is that this correction leads to courage. Wallace had this kind of courage, and I believe King David had it also. Remember when he lopped off Goliath's head and then ran around the countryside dragging this huge head by the hair? All of Israel's courage rose to ward off their enemies. The songs spread: "Saul killed his thousands, David his tens of thousands."

We know that this was historically the event that initiated the thrust of David's reign over the nation of Israel. The nation rose and became so highly encouraged that it became one of the most powerful nations in the world at that time, even though the population was small in number and insignificant in geographical possessions.

Are you an encourager? Are you the kind of person who, just by your presence, spurs people to be filled with courage to face life? Or are you the kind of corrector who discourages people?

Correction isn't intended to rob people of their courage to face life. True spiritual criticism leaves the hearer with greater courage and inspires profound confidence in God's work in our lives.

One of the evidences often cited for Jesus' resurrection from the dead is the amazing change in the level of courage displayed by the disciples and other early followers after Jesus' postresurrection appearances around Jerusalem. These men who had been cowardly, egotistic, striving, thieves—and all at the same time they were learners. They rose to a level of faith that they were willing to give their lives at any second for what they had seen. They were filled with courage.

In every one of the postresurrection encounters Jesus had with them, they were first struck with absolute terror. Christ's presence in and of itself was a correction. They had already begun—like sheep—going the wrong way. As Jesus appeared to them on several occasions, the Bible says they were terrorized, their hearts were warmed, their eyes were opened, and they had moments of clarity all caused by the correcting Christ himself.

But they didn't stop there. Everyone Jesus encountered after his resurrection was filled with courage to face life. Jesus' postresurrection encounters were filled with both encouragement and correction. This is the pattern to powerful discipleship.

It isn't just others who are to criticize us. We'll later learn the importance of self-criticism. Paul warned us rather sternly in his first letter to the Corinthians (chapter 3) to judge ourselves so that we don't end up being judged by others. When you judge yourself, do you follow the positive purpose of correction, or are you one of those who think it's spiritual to dismantle yourself? Or are you one who lives accidentally, letting childhood pain and injury, disappointment, and harsh words from others dictate how you view yourself?

We're expected to judge ourselves, to correct ourselves, and to admonish ourselves. But we're to be as gentle and careful with ourselves as we would expect others to be. "Sins and mistakes are better learned from than punished" is the saying I want to go with to my grave.

There is a central theological truth that pinpoints the need for criticism. Humanity is not complete. Humanity is in process. The following is an interesting summary of this truth. Emil Brunner wrote, "Figuratively speaking, God produces the other creatures in a finished state; they are what they ought to be, and this they remain. But God retains man within His workshop, within His hands" (Emil Brunner, *Man in Revolt* [Philadelphia: Westminster Press, 1939], 97).

Can We Live Without Criticism?

WOULDN'T IT be nice to have, say, a five-year reprieve from anything but praise? No doubt a reprieve from scrutiny could be a good thing for all of us from time to time. But a life without criticism is not a happy one.

I had a high school friend, Bill, who illustrated the deep need to be corrected. His mother abandoned the family when his sister was born and he was two. To make things worse, his father was an alcoholic country musician. No one ever corrected Bill, and he loved to get into trouble. I think the attention made him feel secure. Throughout his life he has been a prime example of a troubled soul craving correction.

The Bible affirms that we have a conscience, the part of us that self-criticism comes from. The Bible authors tried to prevail over our remarkable tendency to silence our conscience. We need self-criticism. Yet sometimes our conscience is off balance, and it's then that we need outside correction.

A number of years ago I heard a lecture by a psychologist explaining how as adults we parent ourselves just exactly the way we were parented as children. He persuaded us that we have a little child inside our minds who runs things. I have found it to be true again and again. The way we were criticized in childhood sets the pattern for our self-criticism for both others and ourselves. But the sad part is that if we've not had healthy criticism, we're at a loss sometimes as to how to live in hard times. And sometimes we buckle in life when the pressure is on, because we've not been trained with the kind of correction that gives us character.

What if we've been raised in the new "self-esteem"-based school curriculum? The premise of this approach is that any negative input will cripple a student, that if a person feels good about himself or herself, he or she will be able to face life with greater fulfillment.

The truth, however, is that this kind of nonperformance-based education leads to creating mental cripples who don't know how to face the skirmishes life brings our way.

If a person is never criticized at home for fear his or her ego would wither, he or she often ends up feeling unloved. This fact has always amazed me, but it's true. A life without criticism sets one up for low self-esteem. A pampered child from today's social experiments often feels unloved, like my friend Bill.

Seattle, my home, is a liberal yet adventurous city. Sometimes I think anything novel is worth a king's ransom in this city. My son played a lot of sports as a kid, and I loved watching him practice and play.

I still grin when I recall one of his basketball leagues. They didn't keep score. No, I'm not kidding. Some of the mothers had taken control of the league and convinced everyone that little guys shouldn't have the pressure of the scoreboard.

One evening I just had to ask one of the leaders how they became so opposed to competition. I knew I was treading on dangerous ground, but I was curious.

"June, how do you like the game?" I asked awkwardly.

"Isn't it nice just watching the kids have fun for fun's sake?" she replied, giddy with enthusiasm.

"Don't you notice that they're still keeping score?" I said. "It's human nature. I have to know—what is the basis of this whole idea of no score board? I mean, I love people. I'm an encourager most of the time, but this just seems kind of silly." I stopped as another pointless basket was being cheered.

"You wouldn't understand. You guys think you're finding meaning in who you beat. But life is about more than winning. We think sports should be for the team experience and fun. So many children feel belittled by scores and such. The point is to just play and care about one another. I was constantly criticized growing up. Even though I achieved, I was compared to my sister and cousins, and it really made life miserable. So I've found along with others that a world without ridicule is the most human one."

"Oh, I see" was all I could force out of my mouth.

The season was the silliest thing you've ever seen. The boys hated it and kept score on their own despite its harm to their souls. The bad players were still bad, and the good players tried to keep the ball from them. But a few of the "competition haters" were in heaven with this social experiment, blind to the poor reception the kids had to their idea.

If I recall properly, this scheme lasted two seasons. Then to keep the parents coming out with the kids, they had to keep score, even though they didn't keep season records. Everyone was a champion at something without any required performance level. Yikes!

Is Evaluation Toxic?

Being correctable is one of the highest traits of a wise person, according to Proverbs 15:5. The word for "correction" in this verse is associated with being disciplined with a firm hand. It has an ancient connection with the word "peacock." I suppose the peacock got in there with the idea that criticism brings color into your life! Primarily the word is a call to listen intently to criticism in order to achieve all you would dream. After all, a person who receives only praise loses touch with reality.

Comparison admittedly is not a healthy way to find your identity. We find who we are by surrendering all of who we are to God and his vision for us. But none of us can make that journey without some evaluation coming our way.

I've known people who conduct themselves in such a way that they're free from any threat of criticism. Denial is a great hiding mechanism, a talent that's perfected by those who hide from analysis. I once tried to help a gambling addict get free of his addiction. He was a master at denial and blew up with any hint of criticism. His tactic was well learned over the years. He simply wore out his critics with denial. Sadly, however, his problem didn't go away.

No one can grow or stay free without loving input. If we're not open to criticism, we'll find ourselves adrift in the sea without any idea of how we got there.

The Heart That Avoids Criticism

Twenty years ago I joined a group of Seattle ministers in setting up a meeting with a church pastor whose congregation was growing but was promoting some troubling heresies. The meeting started off with charming interaction—but when we began to ask questions about issues of how people were treated, their non-Trinitarian leanings, and other issues, the leader exploded. He thanked us for coming but staunchly informed us that God had already spoken to him and that he didn't need a bunch of Pharisees to advise him.

Eighteen years later, most of us who had concerns were strapped with the task of helping couples who had been destroyed by a leader who could not be criticized. He had led the large congregation into what amounted to spouse-swapping. Tragically, only a few made it out intact. If only he had been a leader who could face criticism, a great work would have continued.

My mentor helped me work through the first few books I wrote. I loved seeing him every other month, but I really hated it when we pulled out my manuscripts. He said his main task in my life was to help keep me tender by his loving criticism, because pastors of large churches have a way of hiding behind their position and avoiding being told they have weak spots. Fortunately, he did keep me tender. I didn't always agree with his assessments, but I did learn that it was normal and essential to be corrected if I were to write anything worthwhile.

My son had a teacher whose goal was to have every student get an A. And most of them did, except the ones who really put in the effort *not* to. The A meant nothing to the kids, though. It affected them something like a guitar string that's not brought tight enough to be in key. Their educational time sounded out of tune.

Earning the Right to Be Heard

As a pastor I've had plenty of criticism, and in the end it's all been profitable. I remember one couple who confronted me about a curt correction I had given a young man in one of our Bible study services. I realized that I had really been too cranky, and I didn't want to hear anything about it after the service. I knew when they reached me that I was going to have to come down off my pompous perch.

"Pastor, can we offer you our feelings?" the husband said.

"Well, of course," I replied politely. Inside, though, I was saying *Yeah, right*.

"We think you were far too harsh to that young man, and that's not like you. Do you need a break?" And then he added the one thing I hate hearing the most when I'm being confronted: "We want you to know we're praying for you."

I don't know where the words came from, but I said, "You know, if you don't like the way I lead, you can find another church!"

"No, we're not going anywhere—this is our church as much as yours," the wife said. "And you should listen to us."

I started laughing, losing my breath for a moment. Then we all started laughing and hugging each other. And none of us ever dwelled on that challenging moment again.

I still think of this era in my life, when my desire to avoid criticism could go so far as ending relationships. If you're never criticized, you grow flabby, sloppy, and—well, pompous. I know I suffered a great deal as the pastor of a very large church from not being corrected. People would not correct me because either they were afraid of me or they couldn't believe I could be human. We all need to earn the right to be heard—and accepting criticism is an important part of that process.

Missing the Riches of Criticism

Let me outline what I think we've learned so far about what happens when you're not criticized:

- You get lazy and sloppy.
- Your self-esteem is low due to being left untried.
- You become foolish and have an underdeveloped sense of judgment.
- You become prideful and pompous.
- You soon can't hear the Holy Spirit.
- You avoid challenges.
- You actually stop trying new things for fear of discovery.

- You're unprepared for a life charted with pitfalls.
- You have retarded social skills.
- You have diminished intelligence.
- You become rebellious and deny God's lordship often.
- You're never the best you could be.
- You never learn the joy of working with a team.
- You one day discover you're not the center of the world.
- You make the same mistakes over and over again.
- You run the risk of becoming self-destructive.
- You believe toxic untruths.
- You're a horrible model for those around you.
- You're laughed at in derision at some point.
- You make less money.

What about Hidden Faults?

Is it possible to be doing wrong and have no idea you are? Yes, I think human experience would support a yes on that.

David's prayer in Psalm 19 included the plea "Forgive my hidden faults." This is a fascinating prayer. He wanted to take care of those occasions when he was certain he could be doing and be living in self-deception. Is it possible to fool yourself and no one else? Again, I think our experience would call us to say, "Yes!" So what can we do?

David prayed that God would reveal hidden sin so he could flee it. He set his heart to hear outside his own experience, knowing that he could be offending God and not even know it. Any married man hates these words from a woman's mouth when asked what's wrong: "Oh, nothing!" We know we've failed again and can't even see where.

Loving Is Confronting

Kids who are corrected know they are loved. Children left to their own development become crippled by the indifference. And usually pampered or overly indulged children can have questions as to whether they are loved or not.

I have found that as parents, we can gain a great deal by taking on new paradigms in our task of developing new lives. We should from time to time see ourselves as mentors to our children. Often they simply need a guide—but all children need to be evaluated and confronted.

Confronting the Fake Within

I spend a good bit of time tuning my guitars, but no matter how well I tune my instruments, there's one chord that will never be in tune—the D chord. The harmonics on a guitar's fret board just can't get a perfect pitch on a D chord.

Our lives are much like that. Then imperfect parts of our lives are left there, I'm certain, to keep us humble and seeking God. Correction brings a reminder that we still can play out of tune and that only one person plays with perfect harmonics—God.

Criticism is often the tool God uses to keep us moving in the right direction. I once wanted to be a doctor. I knew I would make a great one. One problem, though—I didn't take any biology or chemistry classes. Why not? I just didn't have the aptitude in those areas, so I hated them.

When I met with the premed advisor, he immediately noticed I didn't have any science courses. My bachelor's degree was in literature. He said candidly to me, "I don't think you're made to be a doctor. I encourage you to find another calling. You won't make it here, kid."

I was hurt by his abruptness. But now that I look back, this man closed the door solidly enough that I found my way to my real calling. To find your calling, you must go through the arduous passageway of criticism. You find who you are by facing who you are not—and this process requires criticism. If we avoid it, we begin living in fantasies. Criticism pushes us to reality. Avoiding it leaves us with nothing but talk.

CHAPTER

Leaders and Criticism

ODAY'S WORLD is not leader-friendly. My friends in Australia have an idiomatic expression for their culture's tendency to tear down leaders. They call it the "tall poppy syndrome." They mean by this that the masses like to clip down anyone who excels. The habit of many is to hold high achievers in the grip of suspicion. I detect that this syndrome is becoming truer and truer in North America as well.

> Then I heard a loud voice in heaven say: "Now have come the salvation and the power and the kingdom of our God, and the authority of his Christ. For the accuser of our brothers, who accuses them before our God day and night, has been hurled down."
>
> REVELATION 12:10

Scrutiny of leaders is today aimed at far more than their skills or moral lives. They are also held in derision for the sheer fact that they have had the audacity to try to lead. The press seeks to add its part in bringing them down. And unfortunately, the leaders' own behavior brings them down sometimes. Lapses in character in leaders feed all our critics.

Growing numbers of church leaders are stepping down from the ministry. Sometimes it's due to burnout from overcommitment. But more often than not, it's the gnawing fatigue from an environment of hypercriticism. And unfortunately, I don't see many denominations stepping up to support their pastors. It's as though denominational leaders fear the criticism of the saints in the ranks rather than value the contribution of their leaders. The true assets of any Christian organization are not the money in the bank or the facilities they own, but the quality of leaders they have developed.

We can't afford to place church leaders above criticism any more than we can afford to beat them down. Congregations and Christian organizations must be taught to criticize biblically. We're losing some of the best and brightest in church leadership as they move on to other fields. Petty complainers who are not required to follow protocol in challenging leaders are paralyzing churches by the hundreds.

One of the requirements before becoming a leader in any church should be a course in how to give and receive biblical criticism. Too often high-minded critics sound as though they are spokespersons for the Holy Spirit, but in reality they speak only for their own fears and limited perspectives. Criticism can be a dear friend to churches and leaders, but it becomes a foe when mismanaged even by well-intentioned people.

Leaders, on the other hand, must learn to recognize their need for criticism to remain balanced. This isn't always fun. Nor is it always easy to discern a false from a true critic. This challenge reminds me of the parable that Jesus told in Matthew 13 about the weeds among the wheat. We as humans can't always tell the difference between a good "plant" and bad. That's why it will be the angels' work at the end of the world to separate them. Similarly, we can't always recognize constructive correction from nonconstructive. Leaders, more than any other people, must remain open and slow to react to criticism.

A woman leader in one of my church starts came to me and said, "Pastor Doug, you never mention great women of faith in the Bible in your messages. I've been noting your references and would encourage you to consider doing a series of messages on great women heroes."

"Are you saying I sound like a chauvinist?" I responded, folding my arms. "If you are, you're very wrong."

"No, I'm saying you're sounding like one by virtue of your silence about women," she answered with a polite and warm smile, "and it's troubling me."

The aspect I hated most about this encounter was that I'm definitely not a chauvinist and have worked hard many years to promote and develop women leaders. And second, I knew she was right. I just couldn't get myself to admit it. It was as if I had a five-ton gorilla sitting on my responder.

"Thank you—I'll pray and consider your concern," I said, ending the conversation.

I was planning my next four months' speaking calendar that very week. As I prayed about the material I should cover, I realized I had to do a series on women of faith. And it was clear to me that my friend's criticism was timed so well that it must have been nothing less than a gift of the Holy Spirit.

Proverbs of Reproof

I've highlighted a group of verses from Proverbs in my Bible, and I review them at least once a month. I call them a *leader's curriculum for growth*. I've had to fight a war of unjustified criticism many years, so I've sought biblical guidance in this area. I realize it becomes easy to neglect reproof just because of past hurts from unnecessary criticism. A regular reading of the verses of Proverbs dealing specifically with criticism keeps my heart softened. I encourage you to do the same.

Evaluate your life as a layperson in leadership or a professional leader in a church with the following proverbs lying before you. Learn them well. Realize that there are great rewards and benefits for a leader who is open to life-giving correction.

- My son, do not despise the Lord's discipline and do not resent his rebuke, because the Lord disciplines those he loves, as a father the son he delights in.—Proverbs 3:11–12
- Rebuke a wise man and he will love you.—Proverbs 9:8
- He who listens to a life-giving rebuke will be at home among the wise.—Proverbs 15:31
- A rebuke impresses a man of discernment more than a hundred lashes a fool.—Proverbs 17:10
- Rebuke a discerning man, and he will gain knowledge. —Proverbs 19:25
- Better is open rebuke than hidden love.—Proverbs 27:5

Judgment vs. Encouraging Admonishment

Many congregations have been hurt time and again by leaders. It's very difficult to heal congregations, so the healing is often left undone. Wounds develop that infect and weaken God's work. When they have been betrayed, congregations go through grief and depression much as individuals do.

Usually innocent leaders get the punishment for others' sins. It's important to understand that biblical admonishment is not punishment. You may remember that Jesus said, "Don't judge." Rather, we should spur one another on to be Christlike. Judgment is deciding what another's punishment should be. Judgment is the belief that a person is only what he or she does wrong. Forgiveness, on the other hand, is remembering that each of us is always much greater than what we do wrong.

Friendly criticism is a loving adjustment without recrimination. True criticism expects that improvement will come. It also believes God is at work in the recipient and that God can be trusted with the outcome of the correction.

I've often heard the phrase "Consider the source" in reference to discordant comments. This statement has some merit. If people who make no contribution to the organization criticize a leader, their criticism should be muted. And those who leave an organization should be allowed to give feedback as they leave—but if they're not willing to go through the arduous task of being part of a growing church through both the good times and the bad, they've forfeited their right to criticize.

Let's look further at the differences between judgment and biblical admonition.

- Judgment identifies the person totally by his or her sins or wrong deeds. Admonition realizes that one's misdeeds are but a small part of what he or she is as a person.
- Judgment wants to set the punishment for the crime and have the person's value end there. It's based on the false belief that if we could just find out who's wrong, things will be right. Forgiveness knows we're all wrong in various respects.
- Judgment rejects the person totally because of his or her errors. True biblical admonition embraces the person for the journey ahead.
- Judgment can be based on general and vague accusations that may never go away. True biblical admonition is based on specific facts. In other words, if you're going to accuse someone of being prideful, you had better be able to point to clear, specific instances when this pride has been seen in action.
- Judgment seeks to hurt rather than heal. This practice is built on the notion that the person needs to hurt to improve.

- Judgment offers no way out. True admonition offers steps beyond the error.
- Judgment always looks backward and seeks to rehearse or rewrite history. Biblical admonition looks forward to a bright future. It finds the future friendly and filled with possibilities for the person being criticized.

Why Do Leaders Hate Criticism?

Most leaders are on overload. This, plus the fact that criticism is the most emotionally draining experience a leader faces, makes criticism feel like a kamikaze attack. The sad result is that we leaders get good at ducking criticism. Whether you're a politician, a PTA leader, or a church leader, you must resonate with this fact. I can guarantee you that most leaders today are going to overreact to criticism, because frankly they're over-assaulted. Here are some points that are true about criticism with regard to leaders.

- Criticism of leaders is far too prevalent.
- Criticism on the job is in fact dangerous to a person's health. I have noted that the health of many key leaders in churches breaks down during seasons of criticism.
- Often criticism is based simply on things like preferences of music style and other trivial concerns. This kind of careless treatment of leaders weakens the fiber of any organization. Higher goals and higher aims must be the focus of good ministry, not petty preferences.
- Leaders are often the focus of people's fear about the future. The world is uncertain, and many look to leaders for security. Leaders have zero control over the future, so they are often assaulted for not meeting expectations that all will go well.
- Leaders overload on criticism when there is too little positive feedback in their lives. My personal feeling is that board

members should offer feedback within a set method that supports sound correction but filters needless rebuffs. Boards should also set up ways to formally take criticism or thanks from the congregation.

- The loneliness that leaders experience often makes criticism deadly.
- The fear of failure in leaders is often crippling, making any comments of disapproval suffocating. We must learn to see failure as part of the pathway to success.
- The need to be liked can paralyze a leader. Many of the people they lead don't like leaders. The ground upon which leaders must stand is that they are seeking God's approval. And criticism may be God's way of leading them to honor him in a bigger way.
- If Christian leaders don't find counselors or allies to help heal the constant wounds from criticism, the outcome is usually tragic.

★ ★ ★ ★ ★

Unhealed wounds can cause leaders to think in combative terms. The fear of being hurt again can create almost paranoid behavior in a believer. The paranoid belief that those who agree with him or her are good and that those who don't are the enemy can end a ministry. If a leader finds them getting commutative, it's a sure sign that there's some need for healing.

I have plenty of past hurts. Anyone who has been hurt would be an amazing person if he or she didn't have more pain than needed. I find that past pains and hurts cloud my perception of present criticism. I've learned to count to 100 before I respond to attacks. This gives me time to make certain I am not letting past pain bleed over into the moment.

Sometimes I'll respond with a short question. But many times I'm tired and embarrass myself. There are times when you don't want to be the next leader in line for "help."

Leaders are all human. And even the best require grace from their followers, especially when in the caldron of criticism. A leader's fatigue can cause judgment to slip. And the very time a leader needs to be confronted is the time he or she is least likely to be able to entreat it with joy. Most churches today overcommit their leaders. If a leader is tired and already putting in eighty hours a week, criticism from boards or church members can be very crippling.

I know a leader who could not accept any critique from any other leaders—ever. If the budget was criticized, he encouraged the objecting board member to leave the board. The board was required to have a unified response to everything. Consequently, if there was any critic who didn't agree with the pastor, he or she was forced to have his or her vote unheeded—and not only that but to submit his or her resignation. This group, as you can well imagine, experienced a great deal of pain and agony at the hands of this leader.

On the other hand, in one of the churches I've consulted the pastor was involved in a very serious car accident, which altered his personality significantly. In an attempt to find his way back to effectiveness, he became imbalanced by trying to prove he was recovered. His effort to overcome the depression and the debilitating effects of the wreck was admirable, but it threw the group into further instability. Leaders in severe pain or discouragement hardly ever lead well. My friend should have stepped aside. We both agreed he was a bad fit for the church and vice versa. A leader in his frame of mind is hard on a congregation, too. He put off his critics when they confronted him face-to-face, going on the attack so often that the criticisms escalated due to his inability to hear.

I wish I had been introduced into the situation soon enough to encourage the people to take into account the effects of the wreck on their pastor. Depression nearly always follows injuries like those he experienced. These critics needed someone to call them to compassion and to seek help for their shepherd. The pastor needed to listen and trust others, but in his depressed state it was very difficult.

Sadly, the situation was irreconcilable. My advice was for the pastor to start another church and to bless the congregation he was leading as he departed. Once criticism begins to get out of hand in a Christian organization, the scene can be like the frenzy of a wild dog pack attacking a rabbit.

Criticism should be a face-to-face encounter. Receiving secondhand criticism is very fatiguing. Jesus made this clear in his teaching that if you find fault with another, you're required to confront him or her. (In our chapter on protocol, *How Does Jesus Criticize?*, we'll learn the skills of criticism and amplify this point.) Jesus commanded that if it's clear that they aren't hearing you, then you go to the church officials, and then there will likely be a confrontation of monumental proportions.

Solving matters of criticism requires humility. Leaders have to seek win-win scenarios as much as possible. Criticism should never lead to agony or a breach in fellowship. It's worth the effort to find the way to peace. This kind of harmony requires a willingness to meet each other somewhere in the middle.

I encouraged my friend mentioned above to spend a week alone making lists of ways to resolve things peacefully. I hoped he would resign himself to bless the church and move to start another one across town. I felt all involved needed to admit culpability in letting the criticism get out of hand. My excessive optimism was crushed again. He left the church in great disharmony.

Criticism must be managed for the cause of Christ to advance properly. And criticism can bring a win-win situation if it's viewed as normal and friendly.

How Criticism Should Work in Your Organization

The format for criticizing a leader should be established beforehand. As I said, I believe any board or Christian organization should be taught how to bring admonition or reproof to a leader. They shouldn't stop there, however. They should teach and model before the church how to bring criticism.

The following is an outline of points that should be the criteria for criticizing a leader. These are the bases of true biblical criticism in the church and in any other organization.

1. All criticism must be based upon an agreed list of expectations of the leader. These expectations should be known widely in the church. And in today's world, the expectations of the leader's wife and family should be known as well. There should be nothing expected of them other than what the rest of the church must meet as well.

   Of course, by this we're talking about a job description—and not just a list of activities to be carried out but also measurements that describe how the congregation's leaders will know they're succeeding. The number of Christian organizations that don't have job descriptions astounds me. If clear job descriptions aren't available, criticism will proliferate. The list of expectations should be very specific, listing not only hours put in but also number of calls made, specific tasks, the number of sermons, the length of sermons, hours made available to counseling, and more. All of these are essential to assure that any criticism is based upon the right criteria.

2. All criticism should be based on a strategic plan. Leaders in any organization should not be whimsically criticized for the subjective wishes of the group. A strategic plan listing aims for its leaders is essential to a group's health. The entire church should know how these aims will be achieved, and leaders should be evaluated as to how satisfactorily they work toward this strategic plan.

   And personally, I think congregations should be evaluated as to how they respond as well. No congregation should criticize a leader if at least half of them aren't volunteering at least an hour each week. I find any criticism of a leader from someone who does not volunteer his or her time ludicrous.

3. There should be clear patterns of rest and recreation. In other words, the expectations should allow for breaks that maintain balance. I'm talking about vacations here. Ministry breaks for leaders are essential for success. Restoration is a valuable investment a church makes available to its leaders. Churches who burn their leaders out, drain them, and then criticize them must be very disappointing to Christ.

I know a church that receives a special offering each year to be spent on their pastor's lengthy vacation time. This has paid off great dividends for the congregation. Pastors should also be invested in management skills, pastoral ministry skills, and professional improvement. Criticism without this kind of investment is a miscarriage of congregational or Christian life.

4. Criticism of the toxic variety can be avoided if the pastor has a small accountability group of whose existence the congregation is aware. They don't necessarily need to know the names, but they need to know they're there. Simply having a board is not satisfactory. The board should stick to the business of the organization and evaluate the pastor on the basis of carrying out business. A small accountability group, on the other hand, can speak into the personal areas of a pastor's life. I have found that when this is taken care of, a great deal of meaningless criticism can be abated.

5. There should be a clear understanding of the difference between important and unimportant criticism. If a pastor is criticized for the car he or she drives, shame on the church organization. If the pastor is criticized for inappropriate behavior toward members of the opposite sex, he or she must be admonished.

6. There can be a regular forum for feedback regarding a leader's performance. Sending out forms to the church asking for

input on the overall aspects of the church's ministry is vital. Regular and meaningful outlets for feedback can avoid needless criticism as well. Many churches hold "forums" after services to collect questions or criticism.

7. Regular reviews of leaders by the board and the immediate teams of any leader are vital. Once again, living deliberately beats living accidentally. Living accidentally is sure to lead to a poisonous environment.

8. Criticism can be tolerated if equal and regular public appreciation is expressed for the pastor's work.

9. Expedient and clear outlines must be in place regarding what will happen in the event of a leader's misbehavior. A leader who misbehaves morally should be removed and a plan of restoration established. There should be little time available for wringing of hands, deciding what to do. A leader's knowledge that misbehavior will be handled quickly, fairly, and lovingly can be a powerful deterrent.

★ ★ ★ ★ ★

Criticism must be viewed as only part of the process of problem solving. One denomination I enjoy working with has a group of peers. Pastors review all claims of misbehavior quickly. This allows issues to be handled outside the rancor of built-up hostilities. And they can take an objective look at the problem and contend for the right path.

Leaders will be criticized. So if you are one, expect it—it's normal. And an organization's future effectiveness lies vulnerable to how criticism is entertained. I have observed, and so have business consultants, that runaway criticism of overseers is scraping the flesh right off our organizations.

But in the end congregations need to be criticized and so do leaders. Our call is to handle business biblically.

Healing from Damaging Criticism

PEOPLE ARE FRAGILE. Big burly men try to fool us with their bravado, but even they are built with delicate and fragile souls. Each of us is a work of art. We're each a complex mixture of attitudes, past experiences, and present fears. Damaging criticism has injured most of us.

I have an aunt who called me "Chubby" and still does. I'm still affected by it at times. But I've learned to make it a positive memory to remind me of how wrong people can be about me. I had a friend who loved to go out of his way to point out how poorly I typed or that I got numbers turned around. This criticism frankly hurt me, though I laughed. The good news is that if we live deliberately, we can be healed of this pain.

I have a friend who has a very lucrative executive placement business. He spends hours studying and assessing his clients. I asked Dave for some clues in hiring personnel.

He said, "The eyes are like billboards. If you look closely, you can see a person's life right before your eyes and can possibly predict his or her performance. You can see hurt. You can see courage. And you can even tell someone who'll quit when the heat is on."

I took Dave's advice and learned to study the eyes of those I've been asked to help. I've learned that there's no past event that shows in the eyes more than harsh criticism. It angers me to see the lasting effects of careless attacks in the home. The soul is crushed under verbal abuse.

I had a friend in high school whose father had abused him for years. He was violent himself, and his eyes betrayed how raw he was inside. His exterior confidence was a compensation for his low view of himself, caused by many beatings with a belt but, more so, also with words that cut more deeply than a knife.

I saw Dennis a few years ago. He's an overachiever now, but he lacks the ability to enjoy his success. His posture and the way he talks show he is not free of the long sessions with belts and sticks and words that tore him open.

All abuse cripples its victims. Usually verbal abuse isn't thought to be as serious as physical abuse, but it's every bit as dangerous, causing even deeper damage. Time doesn't heal all wounds, and it never heals the damage of toxic criticism.

None of us have to think very hard to remember someone who used words like machetes on us. Some too weak to run from verbal abuse get trapped in fear. They're either too young or have their financial well-being in the hands of an abuser, so they stay put, imprisoned by the pain. Most of us would do just about anything to flee words that rip the soul apart. But the feeling of powerlessness keeps many prisoners in the clutches of verbal destruction.

One ironic fact about those abused is that they often become abusers themselves. Verbal abuse is contagious. Families of abusers breed more abuse. This is one of the reasons extreme efforts to stop this form of abuse are necessary.

It's possible to be healed of damaged emotions. It never happens accidentally, though. Like all healing, it must be handled deliberately. And the healing needs to be given with skill and compassion.

How Does Healing Start?

Healing starts with a proper diagnosis. Once the diagnosis is confirmed, the prescription follows. Accepting the fact that you've been damaged by verbal abuse is a vital start to walking away from the lingering pain. Healing comes with surrender to the Great Healer. It takes courage to admit that we've been victimized. The embarrassment of being a victim of an abuser keeps most people locked up without healing. So once the diagnosis is found, the prescription can begin if and only if you admit you've been hurt.

Wounds from harsh words require the careful assistance of a trained healer. Counselors and psychiatrists have given their lives to halt injury to broken souls. It's just plain hard work for the patient to contend for his or her recovery. It takes learning to hear a different voice within yearning to be healed.

I counseled a man in his thirties whose father abused him emotionally as a young boy. His mother eventually removed him from this dangerous environment. The fact that the father was looked up to by a whole city made the pain worse—he was a local television personality. One day he asked to speak with me after a meeting I was leading. He hadn't heard from his father in years, his only memories being of his dad's calling him a little snake, stupid, "big head," and any number of profane names. He could hardly get the words out as he told me about his first seven years of life.

It took several conversations for the man to accept the damage that had been inflicted upon him. He had become the classic overachiever but inside was still the one described by his father's words. Finally he accepted the truth and moved on to finding what his

Father in heaven said about him. He flourished with his new identity and began to experience the best years of his life.

I taught him how to take Paul's and Jesus' prayers and see God the Father praying those prayers over his life. I had learned that the realization that Jesus is singing and praying for us is a powerful antibiotic for poisonous criticism.

My friend's marriage was beyond repair, and he separated from his wife. He moved to Arizona and developed another business there, but we stayed in contact via telephone and mail.

One day I got a five-page letter from him. He said he had finally reached the point at which he could hear what Jesus was praying for him. He wrote, "Pastor Doug, I would have never thought such a simple exercise would open me up to such a wonderful world. I no longer get angry when I see fathers playing with their sons. I see God joining me every day of my life. I know what He sounds like now. I haven't silenced the demons completely, but I've had them drowned out by the new words about me. Thanks!"

Not all hurtful criticism is as easy as my friend's to identify. One of the first students I guided as a pastor came from a wealthy home. He was never physically abandoned, but his father was a controlling perfectionist. Terry's father had been a football hero in college. He had played in two Rose Bowls and never let his family forget it. Terry was an artist. His father often chided him for being a sissy. He just ignored him for years, thinking that would turn him into a real man.

Terry's dad never liked any of his son's friends. He put him down for being clumsy if he tripped or dropped something. He even joked about whether someone so bad at athletics could really be his son. Terry's abusive dad made it known he hated his choice of study, and he informed the whole family repeatedly that if he didn't get straight A's he wasn't getting any money from the family.

His dad wanted Terry to be a pharmacist so he could take on the four stores the family owned. Terry wanted to be in the diplomatic corps and chose a degree in international politics; he also planned to become a professional painter one day. When I met Terry, he was a very bitter person. All I did was ask where his father had gone to college, and his eyes flashed with hatred. Over time I noticed that his face had a permanent look of pain. He was a son who had spent his life in exhaustion trying to please someone who would never be pleased.

Terry poured his heart out to me once, saying, "Do you know what it's like to have straight A's for all your high school and college years and still have your dad say you'll never amount to anything the way you're going?"

I could only respond by saying, "No, I can't imagine the pain. But I know you have a lifetime ahead of you with this situation. You need to get healed first, and then you need to change the source of the poison."

Another student named Steve had been the recipient of the best that elite America has to offer. He had a private tutor for every course so he could excel and be the best possible in it. But Steve just wasn't that kind of person. He excelled at a few things and did tolerably well in others. But despite his family's wealth, he was a kid with average intelligence at best. But he was an extremely happy person. Steve was truly one of the happiest people I had ever met. I asked him one day what gave him his joy.

He answered, "I know Christ's love for me. I know I'm not going to be the topper-most. My parents are committed to giving me every chance. The second factor that brings me joy is that my dad has always told me my best was all he could expect. I know I'll find where I *am* the topper-most. And I know my parents believe that. I can only remember my dad telling me what a great future I had ahead of me. I know I could just drift through school. I can always work with my dad and do very well. But my parents have shaped me by their love and words, and I've always wanted to do the very best I could no matter what lay ahead."

I met Steve's parents at our graduation banquet for college-aged students. They shined with love and joy. His dad said to me, "Steve is a great kid. He's struggled at most things, but there's something in him I've always admired. I didn't have it good at home. My dad was an alcoholic and a thief. I've been cured of the agony of having a dad in prison by loving my son the way I wish I had been loved."

Healing does make a strong showing when we give to others what we wish we had been given. Of course, Jesus said, "Do to others as you would have them do to you" (Luke 6:31). This is a fabulous prescription from the Master Healer.

A young woman in Brisbane, Australia, asked me after a meeting I led how she could forgive her father. He had screamed at her mother all their lives and had said cruel things to the rest of the family. I had been teaching about what God sounded like amid the sea of voices in the world.

Her question was a difficult one for me to answer. Does anyone really know how to tell someone else to forgive? Forgiveness is one of those things that we all wrestle with in agony for ourselves.

What Is Forgiveness in the Face of Abuse?

Sadly, forgiveness is often thought of in terms of overlooking abuse. It can be wise to overlook offenses. In fact, the book of Proverbs says that this is a skill the wise man uses often. But in the instance of abusive criticism, this isn't really what forgiveness means. Abused people often say, "He [She] didn't mean it—I forgive him [her]." But this is not biblical forgiveness.

Healing cannot take place until the crime is admitted. If you're being paralyzed or are in the process of being paralyzed by someone's criticism, the prescription for healing involves confronting the person. There is a time and place for talking to God about the harm and then moving on with forgiveness—forgiving the person before God. But in the case of abuse, there must be a confrontation to be healed.

Forgiveness is never staying within the clutches of abuse or approving the wrong. It doesn't even involve maintaining a relationship with the abuser. Forgiveness can occur even if you decide never to be around the abusive individual again.

Neither is forgiveness feeling good about or safe with someone. You can feel safe with someone only when you are in fact free from harm or risk. But you still can forgive the person in the sense that you refuse to determine the punishment he or she receives and you no longer allow him or her to be a key figure in your life.

- Forgiveness is remembering that everyone is always more than what he or she does wrong.
- Forgiveness is your response to repentance and the desire to change on the part of another.
- Forgiveness is sending sins away from people rather than continuing to define them by their sin.
- Forgiveness is the ability to relinquish the right to determine punishment.
- Forgiveness is valuing yourself enough to confront and state what is right and healthy for you. In this sense, it means not allowing an unhealthy situation to continue.
- Forgiveness is accepting the responsibility for your own safety and releasing the other from that responsibility.
- Forgiveness is putting a stake in the ground, determining that the past will not hold you captive in your future.

Lazy and severely wounded people tend to remain victims. Forgiveness is a demanding exercise. Vengeance and anger are also emotions that are easy to express but leave one empty and exhausted.

I know people who have spent the last twenty years of their lives being wounded and hurt by a church that became abusive. The pastor determined that he was the ultimate authority from God. He removed from the board and other groups anyone who objected to his ideas. This congregation grew rapidly—as do many groups that offer a world that feels like the abuse they experienced as children.

Eventually, however, the egotism of the leader caused the group to collapse. Unfortunately, thirty families had collateralized the church's building. Somehow the leaders of the church had gotten the building financed to 125 percent of its value. When the church went down financially, nearly all of those thirty families were in jeopardy of losing their homes.

Hundreds of people were paralyzed for years of their lives because they had worked so hard for years to be acceptable to the leader. This excessive commitment made it extraordinarily painful to those who had given so much. Many gave up their faith because it was too much for them when they opened their eyes to how extensively they had been abused.

This leader had used a harsh form of silence to keep his people desirous of pleasing him at all costs. If they didn't give what he thought they should, they were excluded and avoided. If they couldn't make certain meetings, their standing in the church suffered. It was an evil environment. His kind of criticism was just as bad as screaming hateful words at the church. And those who did exactly what he wanted were, of course, praised and celebrated. The power of shunning was known in the communities of Puritans in the early days of the United States. Without doubt, silent criticism is a potent killer.

I recently got together with a couple that had escaped this group. I could tell within minutes that even nearly eighteen years after the collapse of the church, they were still living in the grip of victimization.

They shared with me how their trust in God had been broken down by the errors of the leaders. I finally had to say, "Nonsense. You *allowed* yourself to be abused. I know several who left because the abuse was apparent. Why don't you accept personal responsibility?"

I could tell they were both stunned. Then the wife spoke up and said, "Boy—that makes sense!" We prayed together, and the couple left their history in their past. Forgiveness allowed them to move beyond the abuse.

How to Escape Abusive Criticism

There's a tremendous need today for people—especially women and children in abusive relationships—to have the courage to confront and leave. If those in weakened situations could be taught to face abuse decisively, it would be defeated.

Don't think that only women and children suffer abuse. I've also discovered men who have had to put up with abuse from their employers or supervisors and can be just as beaten down. So how does one escape?

First, if you're in a family situation of verbal abuse, I would encourage you to first seek the counsel of your pastor. If the church doesn't take this seriously or can't seem to help otherwise, then I would encourage you to go to a professional counselor. The point of this counsel should not be to discover who's right or wrong but rather to get help in confronting the issue.

Children caught in the grip of an abusive relationship can speak with their teachers at school or with their pastor or other leaders at their church. It's very important that individuals caught in the grip of abuse understand that seeking help is not a betrayal. I've found that all abusers overuse the call to loyalty. And in most dysfunctional families of alcoholics, secrets are kept with a vengeance. There's hell to pay if embarrassing secrets escape the home. If Dad falls down the steps and breaks an arm while drunk, the whole family lies about what happened—or else. And consequently, children live with a great deal of emotional dissonance because of the lies and insanity of alcoholism.

If you observe such an abusive home, you help no one by ignoring it. It will escalate. The Bible encourages you how to handle this: by having a one-on-one confrontation. Of course, you may not be too popular after the conversation, but that isn't the point. We all must contend for health on all levels and have the courage to stop any abuse we see.

I would never continue attending a church where I was treated abusively. If leaders treated me disrespectfully, I wouldn't stay in that church any longer than a couple of weeks. Churches where I'm encouraged not to use my mind or where I feel no empathy are places I run from. Unfortunately, there are more churches like this than I would like to admit.

Being healed of the abusive criticism can mean relocating yourself. You're not responsible to make someone else behave properly toward you—you're responsible to take care of yourself. Your mental and emotional help are in your hands and the Lord's, not someone else's, regardless of how loudly he or she shouts. You're responsible to make sure you're treated with the dignity you deserve.

People who continue in abuse tend to do two things. First, they make excuses for the abuser. They say things like "This isn't what he's [she's] really like." It really doesn't matter what the person is really like—if the person is abusive in his or her criticism, this individual is accountable before God for that, not his or her potential as a human.

Learning to Hear the Holy Spirit's Voice

The process of being healed of the damage of abusive criticism doesn't involve shutting down the voices of your past alone. Healing entails learning to hear God's voice clearly. One of the people I've admired most in my life is a retired preacher who is eighty-five years old. I asked him on one occasion what God sounded like. He chuckled and answered, "He sounds just like me—but a lot smarter."

The elderly preacher also told me that the Holy Spirit speaks only one language. He said, "Remember—there's only one dialect that the Holy Spirit lets himself be heard through. And that's the

Bible. You'll never learn to hear the Holy Spirit any more than your knowledge of the Scriptures." This brief explanation of hearing God's voice made a lot of sense to me. I kept it tucked away in my heart as an understanding whose depths I want to glean all my life.

So What Does the Holy Spirit Sound Like?

Let's outline a few things the Bible teaches us about the nature of the Holy Spirit.

1. The Holy Spirit is always respectful. This is one of many building blocks of evangelism. The Holy Spirit doesn't trample us into believing. The Holy Spirit doesn't use force and demand that people receive Christ. Rather, he respectfully invites us to acknowledge the truth. He lovingly brings before us the facts again and again. He speaks into our emotions and into our intellect, forever presenting the truth but in the most respectful manner. Most all of us bowed our hearts to Christ based on an invitation that came from the Heavenly Father—not on the basis of a demand or on accusations based on fear.

2. The Holy Spirit is always kind. I find many people aren't kind to themselves. I think this is the main reason that people don't believe that God is actually kind to them. The Holy Spirit in his kindness and gentleness is polite. He doesn't offer put-downs or unsavory comments attacking our character and nature. Rather, he's very careful not to embarrass us or make us look smaller in our eyes or the eyes of another. Certainly he does speak the truth, but it's always with good manners.

3. The Holy Spirit is also future-friendly. Because he is God, he is eternal. Never forget past, present, and future mean nothing to him. This is why he can relate to us in a way that's so

profoundly filled with love. He knows the outcome of our lives and how great it will be. Hence, in the present moment, he constantly brings a spirit of hope, knowing the day will be there when we, too, will take on fully the character of Christ. The Holy Spirit will never make us dread our future. He will always fill us with hope and excitement for what lies ahead.

4. The Holy Spirit is also accepting. This doesn't mean approving, but he has a strong inability to reject. One of my friends wrote a song with these profound words: "A cry for mercy always catches His ear." Never doubt it—you will receive grace and acceptance from him whenever you call out to him.

5. The Holy Spirit doesn't deal with punishment. He does deal with restoration and guides us into the restoration of our character when we get lost in fault or sin. But as the Bible says, "There is no fear in love. But perfect love drives out fear, because fear has to do with punishment" (1 John 4:18). He is a broker of hope. If you begin to hear the Holy Spirit, you'll begin to find that the voice of victimization begins to leave your life. Instead of hearing an aggressive teacher say, "You're never going to amount to anything" or a father who maybe rejected you by saying, "You're never going to amount to anything," you begin to hear the voice of the Holy Spirit, who with good manners begins to give you reasons for hope because he's at work in your life.

6. The Holy Spirit speaks gently. He doesn't come with big bands and fanfare or with screams and shouts. He is a quiet, sensitive voice of God at work in your life. This means that sometimes you have to be still to hear him completely. No, he's not like other voices in our lives. He never shouts at you with put-downs. In his quiet, gentle way, he entreats us into his quiet presence to hear him say, "I love you, and I want you."

A Prayer for Healing from Abuse

Prayer is the starting point to rid your heart of the agony of abusive words. I offer the following guide for praying for your own healing from damaging criticism. Jesus taught us to pray, "Forgive us our sins, for we also forgive everyone who sins against us" (Luke 11:4).

A Releasing Prayer

Father, I forgive myself of all wrong as you have forgiven me.
I pray that the abuser would be healed and turned around by your
loving power. I pray for the release of the impact of these memories.
I pray the reactions of cynicism and bitterness would be removed
from my life. I ask for hope and courage to face my pain. I ask you
to repair my broken heart. I ask for guides to help me face this pain.
I ask for faith to defeat fears that keep me in toxic relationships.

Releasing Others in Love

A story from the life of Isaac Newton encouraged me when I first heard it. He had spent years and months working on scientific theories, figuring and refiguring, trying to arrive at some of the final principles of physics. At his side this entire time was his beloved dog. He and the animal had been partners for years. Newton considered him his partner in discovery.

As Newton was completing his studies one evening, he stood up to take a break. The dog rose up with him from under the table and knocked out one of the legs of the table with some force. Several candles fell down upon Newton's papers and quickly reduced them to an ash heap. The papers had been filled with script that included great discoveries in the making. Before Newton noticed the flames, most of the papers were gone. He lunged to the table and put the flames out, but it was too late. His precious thoughts of many months were gone forever.

Newton told this to his friends. He told how he could do nothing but sit down on the floor with tears in his eyes, stroking his beloved friend's fur. He looked in the dog's eyes and said, "Friend, you'll never be able to understand the damage you've done."

I have found that critical abusers are just like Newton's dog. They so often just don't understand the harm they've done. And truthfully, all of us harm others in ways we never realize.

Consider Your Own Sins

Who among us has not hurt others? Sometimes the healing of abuse must acknowledge the harm our own words have caused others. Have you considered those you may have injured with your tongue or your actions? Seeking to amend our verbal damage can help us be healed.

I love the way Jesus reduced all difficult topics down to very stark statements. Remember the ruler who asked Jesus what he had to do to inherit eternal life? Jesus mentioned the importance of obedience to God and then asked him to put his love and obedience into action by giving all he had away. Our spirituality must be expressed in action. And we must make our love for others tangible. The discipline of managing our own tongue and actions is the pathway to total release of the pain and agony we've suffered ourselves.

Friends on the Journey

I'm a strong believer in the Twelve Step concept and in the support groups. Al-Anon and other such groups offer immense help to those who have suffered abuse from alcoholic parents. There's great healing in finding that others have suffered just as we have. Profound steps of growth occur when we interact with people who are a few steps ahead of us in recovering their lives.

If you find yourself paralyzed by the agony of abuse, you may want to seek out one of these groups. Your local phone book will have directions and phone numbers for locations where Al-Anon groups meet. Your local pastor may know as well. You will learn coping skills that others have learned the hard way, and you'll find compatriots in your own struggle to find your way back to health. More than that, you'll find empathy and affirmation in your journey.

All of us hunger to be loved by another. No more agonizing scar comes to our lives than when we're not loved or when we're attacked. All of us have within us an innate need to look to God and hear him say, "Well done, thou good and faithful servant" (Matt. 25:21, KJV). And along the way we mix our cry for the authoritative love of God with strong figures in our lives. These figures can include parents, grandparents, teachers, professors, or employers. When our hopes are dashed not only with the fact that the support isn't there but also the fact they demand what we can't achieve, we freeze.

A professional athlete described to me the pain he carried from his father's failure to take much interest in his baseball career. He told me how he lost a scholarship once while pitching his last game in high school. One of the Big Ten had sent scouts to observe his pitching. His father had promised him that he would be in the crowd that day. But my friend said that when he took the mound, he glanced around quickly—and his father wasn't to be found. He said, "Something inside me just broke. I was overcome with the need to be complimented and cheered on by the person who meant the most in my life. I proceeded to pitch the wildest game of my life. My curves hit the dirt before the plate; my sliders were slow and getting hit out of the park.

"Fortunately, another school invited me to come to its summer training camp. By then, I'd resigned myself to the fact that my father was not going to back my career."

He added with a smile, "In my second year of college I received Jesus Christ as my Lord. I experienced his affirmation. It was an amazing moment after for so long hearing the echo of my father saying 'Your schoolwork is lousy, and you're putting all your hope in this baseball, and you're never going to amount to a good player anyway. You're just not big enough.' I knew my dad just couldn't escape his lock on work. Work was his identity. It was just so difficult for him to pull away and put anyone else even second.

"I learned to forgive him. And I spoke to him about Jesus Christ. I can't say he's become a Christian yet, but our relationship has certainly healed, because I don't expect from him any longer what he either is unable or unwilling to give. It was a nice and quiet affirmation when I signed my first multimillion-dollar contract to call my father and tell him of my accomplishment. I knew that was an accomplishment he could understand."

Courage to Move On

People who have been criticized excessively in their lives can tend to either overachieve or underachieve. My experience has convinced me that those who have been criticized abusively tend to lose courage in facing life. Let me give you a little key I've learned about finding courage again. Try something new. Learn a new instrument, take up a sport like golfing or biking—just do something new.

Along with that, start some new self-talk. Yes, that's a biblical concept. David did it constantly. You remember his saying, "Why are you downcast, O my soul? Why so disturbed within me? Put your hope in God" (Ps. 42:5). Hear God affirm you. Hear him promise your success. Hear him promise restoration of all you've longed for. And in all this, take a conscious stride ahead. Refuse to be locked in the muddle of others' criticism.

Toxic Critics

"**D**RY DRUNKS" are alcoholics who have stopped drinking but wish they hadn't. If they see anyone else consuming alcohol, it frustrates them. Dry drunks reach for criticism to confirm their superior lives. They can't help it if the criticism flows. These are people who are very unhappy, and somewhere in their minds they begin to say, "And the rest of you better not be happy either."

One of the harsh lessons in life is the discovery that not everyone is well intentioned. Honest people easily become prey to manipulators because they have little practice in the nuances of deception. Discernment is a necessary gift to avoid those who encroach upon our emotional health. Learning to say no to toxic critics is one of the most important skills. Saying no to toxic attacks is a vital ingredient of emotional maturity. I was stunned for years every time I ran into a dishonest critic. I just couldn't imagine the lust for power over others that some people possessed.

Growing up in an abusive or addictive home can cause us to "feel at home" with abuse. I have found that women who live in abusive relationships invariably come from abusive homes. They put up with the most awful treatment and think it's normal. But a mature adult can break the cycle of groundless verbal attacks.

It's possible to break lose from a verbal assailant. But first we must see that we're at most levels all right. Toxic criticism finds its way easily into the hearts of those who feel unworthy to be treated with respect.

The first step in resisting a poisonous tongue is to say, "I am created in God's image, and I deserve to be treated respectfully." The second step is to learn the difference between life-giving criticism and destructive criticism. This course almost always requires an ally to help you along the way to health.

Let's take a look at some of the different kinds of toxic critics whom we need to bar from our lives.

Guilt Trips and Controllers

It's impossible to miss manipulators. I didn't have to live too many years before I realized that there are people who genuinely intend ill toward others. The first tool a manipulator will use is comparison with others. He or she accosts unsuspecting victims with statements like "If only you could be like Joe" or "If your work were up to his [her] standards, you'd be getting promoted." The use of comparison is an effective way to beat you down to a level at which you can be victimized.

Wise listeners reject any comparison aimed at changing their behavior. We should be evaluated by competition with ourselves, not the A student across the hall. A wife who compares her husband to her father is usually trying to manipulate the behavior of her husband with toxic criticism.

As a pastor, I've had people come to me and say, "Do you know the pastor at the downtown First Church ends his prayer time with the Lord's Prayer?" The inference is that I'm not as good as the pastor at the other church. And too often I can see that the aim is to manipulate me into doing what he or she wants.

Or how about this one? "I've found that if you sing a bit longer in worship, the power of God can often come down in a really powerful way. We know a church in Louisiana where people reached some incredible new levels of the Spirit because they spent some more time singing. If you could just get an awakening in your heart like Pastor Billy Bob Jumpsuit, maybe we could be on television one day too."

Criticism based on comparison has to be rejected. I decided long ago I wouldn't even bother to be nice to this kind of criticism. I've learned to look directly into the person's eyes and say, "You know, I don't believe in being guided by guilt and manipulation. I have one aim, and that's to honor Christ. I have no desire to be like anyone else."

Another method manipulators use is bringing up past errors—statements like "I wouldn't bring this up if it weren't for the fact that you've done this six times now. And I've seen that you've had to apologize several times about it, too."

Frustrated parents can fall into this habit, making statements like "This reminds me of when you were in fourth grade and you got three F's. You had the same attitude then." Reminding someone of past errors is not valid criticism. This kind of correction has only one outcome—spiritual death.

People never remain the same. We're all "becomers." Valid criticism evaluates us in the moment we reside. And correction should be aimed at the specific infraction. You may recall the apostle Paul's statement that "love keeps no record of wrongs." So go easy on yourself. Let yourself move on to success, and ignore the toxic critics who seek to incarcerate you into someone you have long since ceased to be.

Even in the Constitution of the United States of America, citizens are protected from being prosecuted for the same crime more than once. There's no double jeopardy in Christ's kingdom either.

Toxic criticism not only compares but also defines you by your past errors. Healthy criticism knows always that we're becoming and that everyone is always more than the sins he or she may commit.

The Fearful Critics

I've kept on file a number of "prophecies" or Scriptures people have sent me from time to time. Most can be boiled down to this: "If you don't change, God is going to kill you." We leaders find that anytime there's deep water to be crossed, a fearful critic always seems to be around who knows exactly why we're in trouble.

I faced a battle with depression for several years in my 40's. Psychiatrists have told me that 100 percent of humans face a serious bout with depression at least once in their lives and that about one in five of us are genetically predisposed to debilitating depression that can last a long time.

I decided after escaping the clutches of depression that I needed to report my healing to our congregation. Some say this was a mistake, but afterward several hundred people said they wanted to know how to beat their own depression. This confirmed to me that I had done the right thing.

However, a long-time member of our congregation came to me afterward and said with hand on chin, "I just couldn't imagine that a man of God would admit to such a problem and then seek medical help as well. My husband and I feel your depression is a sign of not living close to the Holy Spirit."

I was tired, so I didn't bother to disagree. I simply said, "Thank you."

Later they sent me a bag of vitamins and herbs. They said in a note, "We have prayed and decided you just need more vitamins and exercise, not a doctor's help." I smiled and thought, *Well at least they care about me. But I hope they don't get hold of someone else.*

Critics like Sharon and her husband view God as our cosmic cop ready to nail your hide to the chair whenever you have a problem. This kind of view of God creates guilt and fear. Criticism driven by fear mars others.

Fearful critics feel that anyone they can't control is dangerous. These critics are looking for a world without ambiguities they can control. Churches are filled with fearful critics. These aren't usually bad people, but they're dysfunctional individuals who usually use confrontation to establish a world that fits their view of themselves and God. You cannot listen to these kinds of critics. Anytime you hear criticism that has behind it the "God will get you" or "You better watch out" tone, it's not legitimate criticism.

Biblically based criticism always leaves the recipient with a sense of peace. There's no ambiguity about the correction—it's specific—and the one corrected is filled with hope. By contrast, pagan views of gods are always loaded with "He'll get you" warnings. Punishment of failure is vital to the pagan belief system.

Unfortunately, sincere people can pick up the habit of "God will get you" thinking. I suspect this line of thought comes from punitive parenting in their formative years. It is easy to feel at home with these fearful responses to life. Habit feels more like a friend than change. It amazes me that some people caught in very unhappy and toxic situations actually prefer their emotional "home" to freedom.

Perfect love casts out all fear, according to 1 John. Fear is never a healthy foundation for growth. Avoid those who use fear to push you to change. Love takes deliberate planning, while fear encroaches upon our hearts and thrives in accidental styles of living.

Passive-Aggressive Critics

Passive-aggressive critics are in biblical terms "backbiters." These people smile to your face but behind your back report how bad you are. They also never express displeasure with you when it counts.

Many well-meaning people develop the habit of passive-aggressive relationships because they fear hurting others. Others use indirect and third-party accusations to control others.

These people wear masks and switch them quickly as though they were thespians in a Shakespearean play. The classic British actors would play two or three roles. Passive-aggressive critics also play several roles. They wear one mask when criticizing a person behind his or her back and another when rallying assailants.

Watch out for these behind-the-back critics. Triangulated criticism is a bad habit and one that rarely is broken. They criticize you by calling others to join in the party. They embolden others to go on the attack while they innocently stand on the sidelines. Most are not bad people—they've just never learned to make their opinions known healthily.

Psychologists refer to a certain class of people who communicate this way as "borderline personality types." A borderline personality controls his or her world by becoming the nerve center for communication at work, in his or her family, and even at church. Such a person keeps fear in the group and develops toxic cultures where secrets are kept at all costs on everyone in the world he or she lives in.

Passive-aggressive people can wear out an organization. They create a communication underworld. This unhealthy criticism breeds paranoia in an organization. Their two-faced approach to life eventually crushes their own lives. These people view all life as a war, and winning this war is the energy that drives their toxic communication. They seek to divide and conquer all around them with their criticism. Never forget that these people will criticize others to your face and will then criticize you to others. Jesus Christ voiced great disapproval for this in his teaching. Jesus reigns in the midst of honesty. His way is truth telling that corrects in love, confidence, and hope.

Analysis reveals that behind-the-scenes criticism is contagious. It also builds institutional paranoia. My approach with a church dealing with runaway anger and distrust is to try to get key people to sit down and voice their feelings truthfully in full view of everyone.

I have an exercise I use to teach groups what triangulated communication looks like and how it corrupts a group. Triangulated communication involves at least three people. The first person is the one being criticized. The second is the one doing the criticizing. The third is the one the critic rehearses the first person's sins with.

Criticism that comes triangularly kills reputations quickly. It's a contagious disease. If a group falls into this pattern, suspicion reigns, and it's very difficult to turn the damage around. And once a group loses trust, its effectiveness grinds to a halt. These unhealthy critics cannot go unchecked, or distrust and abuse will spread.

Insensitive Critics

A number of years ago, I flew back from Haiti through New York City on my way home to Seattle. I had never been to JFK Airport, and it was a shock to a little country boy like me. I spent a night in a hotel near the airport and later the next day took a cab and then a bus from downtown New York City to the airport.

On the bus were weary-looking people from many nationalities and languages. I was flying with TWA on a late-night flight and was very nervous that I would miss it, since the bus stopped at virtually every airline.

Out of insecurity, I walked up to the bus driver about a quarter of the way and asked, "Is this my stop?" He turned to me and said, "No, I'll let you know."

I waited another ten minutes, decided he'd probably forgotten me, so I went up and said, "Is this my stop?" He turned to me and said, "No, Jack—it's not your stop."

Ten minutes later, I was starting to get up out of my seat again when I heard over the bus's sound system loud enough for all the city of New York to hear, "To the man who doesn't know how to read "TWA,' this is your stop! To the idiot from the West Coast who doesn't know how to read, this is your stop." That was my first introduction to New York City bluntness. My self-esteem dropped a notch, but the experience reminds me of people I have met since.

Insensitive critics are those who make it hard for us to hear correction. Now that doesn't mean you shouldn't listen to what they say, but the insensitivity can often be toxic to the learning process.

How do you deal with an insensitive critic? The only way is to be honest. Simply state that you appreciate the information but that the purpose is lost in how it's presented.

A friend, who does his work at Tully's coffee shop, as I do, read me a proposed piece of legislation today. He said, "Look—the feds are going to pass a law to stop telephone marketing. They'll have an agency you can notify to make certain you get no calls. What do you think of that, Preach?"

I thought for a moment and said, "Why do we need a government agency to help us because we're too wimpy to say no? If they do this, next there will be a government agency to help you break up with a girlfriend or help you return clothes that don't fit." If you want to have healthy relationships, you have to step up and speak for yourself. No one else will.

The best way to cope with harsh criticism is to treat others the way you would like to be treated. I believe Jesus had this kind of situation in mind when He said, "Do to others as you would have them do to you" (Luke 6:31). We tend to create the kind of environment that we feed. When you encounter an insensitive critic who responds in the opposite spirit, you'll increase the chances of changing the situation.

Are you sensitive as a critic to those you work with and love? I can quickly recall the many times I've been an insensitive teacher. Insensitive teachers are often those who are frustrated with a process or are irritated with life. People who feel that their frustration gives them a license to abuse others verbally spread relational cancers. They poison the waters of any organization if they're allowed to continue unchecked. Bluntness can be important, but bluntness with destructive tones kills relationships.

Dry Drunk Critics

People who like to criticize others' abilities because they seem to enjoy life more are much like "dry drunks," described at the beginning of this chapter. A dry drunk communicator wants to get the criticism heading toward others before it's discovered that he or she is imperfect. For example, I know many people who feel they can't go to movie theaters. Few of these people are able to enjoy their own convictions with attacking those who don't share them.

Paul warned us about sloppy judging in his letter to the Galatians. He warned against Judases who put others down for freedoms that had been given to them by God. He also told his friends the Corinthians, "All things are lawful for me, but all things are not expedient" (1 Cor. 10:23, KJV). When you impose your personal value system on others without invitation, more likely than not, you become a toxic critic.

Life is to be fun. And life is to be growth. But dry drunk critics see life as a judgment, a fight to avoid addictions. And they see their role as keeping everyone else as clean as they wished they were. Jesus emphatically warned, "Do not judge, or you too will be judged" (Matt. 7:1). And he further warned, "For in the same way you judge others, you will be judged" (v. 2). Being God's spiritual cop is not a wonderful way to live. Healthy critics are peers and fellow muddlers through life—not experts.

I've learned to reject the criticism of people who have trouble with the fact that I'm liberated from religiosity. Of course, we're not to live without restraint. But I think many of our conventions in the Christian world are like straightjackets. I personally prefer joy, liberty, freedom, and creativity. No dry drunk critic is going to inhibit me or keep me from being fully who Jesus made me to be. I would encourage you to be the same way and to avoid any of those around you who fall into this toxic pattern.

In speaking at an event in the Southwest recently, I took time to include a brief recollection of *The Legend of Bagger Vance,* a movie with Matt Damon and Will Smith as the lead actors. The electricity had barely run out of the microphone before a middle-aged man took hold of my arm.

"Do you have any idea the damage you could have caused today?" he said.

I ran my hand through my hair trying to recall what dangerous words I had spoken. I responded to him, "What—do you mean my making fun of my wife's singing?"

"No! You encouraged these leaders to go to movies—that's what I mean!" he announced with huge furrows forming in his forehead.

"You know, I think you could use a few movies so you'd loosen up. You're clearly entertaining a toxic view of God. And you can't imagine adult leaders being capable enough to edit and censor their own world. So let go of my arm, and go ask Jesus about what I've just said." I was glad the encounter was over.

Usually this kind of religious addiction just can't be healed by words. Religion's very nature is argumentation without any sensible purpose.

Envious Critics

Envy caused the first murder, recorded in the fourth chapter of Genesis. Cain wanted what Abel had—God's approval. Under the influence of envy, he decided the way to get favor with God was to take it from Abel. Abel had shamed him by offering the right sacrifice. Cain was an envious critic who was out of control. And our world today is filled with envious critics. They're like lions lying in wait for their prey.

A cousin of mine, Darla, had a terrific job running the finance department of a friend's business. She had been a faithful employee of this company for several years. A month before her demise on the job, she hired a woman named Karen. Karen was incredibly competent, and my cousin was happy to have her working with her.

But no sooner had Karen settled into her job than she began to collect infractions on everybody. She quickly found ways to make friends with the bosses. And having their confidence, she began setting up the opportunity to get what others had and she wanted— a promotion.

She kept track of the length of telephone calls made by Darla and also the number of personal calls. She began to cause questions to arise about my cousin's work. What was really going on in the office was that Karen was successfully stealing Darla's job. Her criticisms were not legitimate. But the way they were presented left questions just the same. The bosses were outsmarted by this underminer.

Envious critics are always like cancer in an organization. They're always unhappy with what they have and want what everybody else has. They usually want to be someplace other than where they are but lack the confidence that they can legitimately get where they want to go. Out-of-control takers are collectors of wrongs and publicize them to get what they want. And their criticism has only one aim—their own personal advancement.

As leaders in churches and businesses, we need to be on the alert to this kind of critic. This is why, again, we come back to the simple protocol rule that no critic should be allowed to run rampant, that the one being criticized is seated in the same room.

It's hard for me to imagine being an out-of-control taker. I can't remember ever wanting what somebody else had. My sins lie elsewhere. I live knowing what I have is always more than I can handle. But I have even run into church leaders and other people who will compromise to get what others have. Out-of-control takers view their role in the church as a means to getting their needs met. And if they see someone advancing in the cause of Christ, they decide that the only way to get their share is to cut the other person down with their mouth.

We've seen the demise of Communism in the last twenty years. This belief system was based on envy and the fear that there's little to go around—that if someone gets a bigger piece of the pie than we do, there will be less for us. But this isn't so. Envious critics must be taught that there's more than enough in God and that advancement does not have to come through illegitimate criticism but by life given to a higher purpose and cause than us. The way to greatness is always based on sacrificing for others, not by making sure we get our fair share.

Jealous Destroyers

Siblings often become jealous destroyers of one another. This differs from being out-of-control takers. Jealous destroyers simply want to stop the joy in others; they get some sort of delight from impeding others' progress.

In the book of Daniel we have a picture of a jealous destroyer who pitted himself against Daniel. Daniel had many critics and made many enemies because his life was full of God's blessing. They watched and waited. Can you imagine a group of people watching day in and day out to see if you would kneel to a false image? When it became apparent that he would not do so, they hurried with reports to King Nebuchadnezzar, saying, "Daniel is not a submitted subject." These were jealous destroyers. They collected, they schemed, they watched, and they reported.

These kinds of individuals destroy families, churches, and businesses. They use criticism in an uncontrolled way. It seems that they just can't help it. These are people who are addicted to chaos, and their critical nature is part of keeping things in havoc.

Unlike envious critics, these critics don't want what others have. They are driven by the desire to make everyone as miserable as they are. They are people who criticize anyone who's finding the fulfillment they've lost.

Punishers

It's hard to imagine, but there are people who just want to criticize you to punish you. Most of us have had occasion to work with disgruntled people who look for ways to put you in your place. This kind of toxic communicator seeks to wear you down so you can realize just how bad you really are. Punishers can even believe they're a gift from God to bring you down to size.

Watch out for punishing critics. You can tell true criticism from punishing criticism by its fruit. True biblical criticism does not seek to punish but rather seeks to enlighten and encourages us to move on.

Critics with Low Self-Esteem

The critic with low self-esteem doesn't feel good about himself or herself and uses criticism of others to give himself or herself a lift. This person has one overriding intention—to have the whole world fall down to his or her level. He or she criticizes successful people for being successful. If someone else is doing well, this person's self-esteem suffers. Such a critic lives by comparison.

Most people will bring their world into alignment with their perceptions of self. And these low-esteem critics are no exception. They don't feel they can climb to new heights or achieve great things, so they bring everyone else down to the level they perceive they're on.

In the 1980s I attended a conference in Chicago hosted by Willow Creek Community Church. I remember the event well because of the great material and a couple of observations I made. I recall a luncheon table conversation that went something like this:

"Hybels is great, but I think they're preaching 'gospel light.'"

"Well, I'm surprised how machine-like everything is."

I couldn't help myself and butted in, saying, "Come on. This is one of the fastest-growing churches of all time. They're reaching more people each month than there are in all six of our churches. Let's not try pulling them down—let's learn and build our own abilities."

How to Know You Have Received Bad Criticism or Good Criticism

You can tell you've received bad criticism by the following:

- You're discouraged.
- You're filled with fear.
- You're angry.
- You don't want to try.
- Your creativity is drained out your toes.
- You find yourself being critical of others.

You can tell you've received good criticism by the following:

- You're encouraged.
- You want to try new things.
- You feel creative.
- You feel accepted.
- You want to give acceptance.
- You have no desire to judge other people.

What to Do When You're Facing Toxic Criticism

Here are seven simple steps to facing down toxic criticism.

1. Be hesitant to believe any criticism that doesn't ring true for you or that you haven't begun being aware of at all, especially when it doesn't have to do with specific acts of wrong.

2. Keep good boundaries around your life. Not everyone who wants to enter into your life to give input should be allowed to. You should treat your life as though you were a gatekeeper. Test to make certain that you want to let the would-be helper in.

3. Never feel crowded or pushed. Accept only input that works at the tempo and speed you can take. Loving communicators understand this and will allow for it.

4. Remember: you have no obligation to hear. If you don't know the messenger, you should first test him or her.

5. Avoid returning insult for insult.

6. You may have to confront the person who is accusing you with the truth. A confrontation can be good. If you're too passive, you may become the unwanted victim of aggressive people.

7. Always tell the truth. Be willing to accept the truth even if the messenger is not credible. Stick to the truth—it matches the facts. Avoid mind reading, judging motives, or imposing expectations, and don't let those be imposed on you.

Family, Marriage, and Criticism

JACK AND JILL were constantly at each other's throats. It was uncomfortable for everyone to be around them. Their communication style was "attack and destroy." If one said the sky was blue, the other would say, "No—it's gray!" in a raised voice.

Jack ridiculed Jill for being overweight. She in turn made fun of Jack's appearance. Neither could do anything without being criticized, it seemed. He said her cooking was too fattening and the house dirty. He felt there was nothing right with anything she did. The attacks were unrelenting.

This was a couple that used criticism as a weapon. Such a brand of criticism tears down the self-esteem of its victims. Sadly, this is the exact aim of many couples. It's easy when you live with someone to cross the line from kindness to hostility. I have decided that everyone on earth is annoying a great deal of the time.

Harmful criticism in marriage is symptomatic of a number of things:

- **Getting even when wounds have not been healed.**
- **Depression.** Depression loves company. Depressed people habitually blame their spouses for their bad feelings.
- **Seeking to be heard.** One mate gets frustrated when the other doesn't listen to his or her complaints, so he or she amps up the volume and pain level in order to be heard.
- **An effort to change the spouse into the other's image.** Accepting a person for who he or she is increases love in a relationship. There's no joy in being someone's "construction project."
- **Guilt.** Blame shifting can be used in a marriage more easily than at the job. If you're criticizing your spouse or children, constantly ask yourself, *Do I feel guilty about my life?*
- **An unfulfilling life.** Could it be your frustration with your life is caused by your need to venture out and try new things yourself?

No Fourth Person in the Trinity

Criticism, even the worst kinds, can be an expression of love, of wanting to see the best for those we care about. There's nothing wrong with that, but criticism aimed at changing another into the image we prefer can destroy important relationships.

Paul wrote, "We all . . . are changed into the same image from glory to glory, even as by the Spirit of the Lord" (2 Cor. 3:18, KJV). And this Spirit, he said, is the spirit of liberty. It's easy to try to replace the Holy Spirit's work in others' lives. It's easy to forget that the Holy Spirit is at work in those we love.

I'm sure you, like me, know at least three people whose lives you could do a better job running than they do. It's so difficult to offer criticism to others without intruding, and it's an additional challenge to trust the Holy Spirit to work once you've spoken the truth.

Fear can sound like the Holy Spirit. Criticism, driven by fear, breeds confusion in relationships. A parent can receive a notice from the school that his or her child is flunking English and explode with criticism. Images of his or her child as a destitute adult unable to read can drive a parent to turn on ungodly pressure. Daily rounds of questioning can cause a child to fail just to make a point.

The Holy Spirit, on the other hand, is patient, kind, and never fears. He inspires hope for the future in place of dissatisfaction with where we are. The Holy Spirit is alive and effective even in the most disappointing circumstances. A wise critic learns to build the skill of trusting God with the work of changing lives. Pray that God will give you trust and confidence in His ability to work in your family members.

I had a friend named Jim with whom I attended graduate school. He was a brilliant straight-A student but had great difficulty trying new things. Jim would have made a great leader, but he just didn't have the self-confidence to express himself.

About eight years after we finished school, Jim visited the church where I was on staff. He hadn't really achieved much, and he knew it. His wife knew it. Everyone knew that something was holding him back. He was one of those tragic underachievers.

Jim had been raised in the home of a pastor. His father was constantly concerned that his children avoid the mistakes that he had made as a young man and longed to see his children achieve great things in life. He allowed his vision for his children to suffocate them without knowing it. I believe Jim's father was a sincere man— but the crippling criticism in his home had kept Jim from trying anything adventurous. He was a man who had two graduate degrees but could hardly manage to keep a job.

"Doug, you've achieved quite a bit, and you seem so courageous, and I envy that," he said to me.

Now, I had never felt that courageous or that successful. But who doesn't love hearing that kind of encouragement? I think he meant that for the most part I had no fear of trying new things. I asked Jim if he had been criticized a great deal as a child.

"Why?" he asked.

I answered, "Because everybody tends to manage themselves just as they were parented. And you clearly demand perfection for yourself—and it's freezing you."

He said, "I know that, Doug, but what can I do about it?"

I paused and said, "You need a new relationship with the Holy Spirit. You need to replace the voice of your father, who was well-meaning but tried to take the place of the third person of the Trinity in your life. In your head you still hear your father's voice trying to direct you by fear of failure. The Holy Spirit wants to give you a whole new source of courage. Learn to know what His voice sounds like. Would he ever berate you? Would he ever say you were incompetent? No! In fact, he said you could do all things through Christ Jesus."

I encouraged him to do a Bible study of the Holy Spirit's attitude toward the believer and to make it a part of his prayer life. This was at least a beginning point in his journey to overcome the spirit of criticism that had limited his life.

The Old Testament has many fascinating words to describe "salvation." One of the most interesting to me is the Hebrew verb *yasha'*, which means to be brought into wide-open spaces. The idea of this word when it appears in the Bible involves God's taking us from narrow, constricting places into wide-open spaces. The Holy Spirit takes criticism and in his sensitive way turns it into a highway to wide-open spaces in life.

The battle was slow, but gradually Jim got over the years of hounding criticism. I was excited to hear that he actually stepped up and presented a message in a midweek service of his home church. His content was extraordinary, and his self-confidence had risen. It was evident that the Holy Spirit had replaced the critic in his life.

Budgeting Criticism

I have a friend who says you should give ten statements of encouragement for every one of criticism. He also taught me that for every one thing I asked for in prayer, I should give thanks for ten things. Criticism requires praise to be effective.

It isn't just couples who squabble in marriages. I find that often children, especially adult children, can become excessively critical of their parents. It's crippling to their parents, who need to be appreciated. After all, every parent would be world class if he or she could just parent by hindsight.

Often someone will ask me how he or she can bring his or her parents to Christ. The first step is by being thankful for all they've done for you. The second is to encourage them by assuring them that they did a good job in your life. The perfect parent has never existed. But most have been loving and more than adequate. Your expressions of love and appreciation will go a long way in pointing your parents to the Lord.

We're all fallen creatures in need of grace. The book of Malachi tells us about the day ahead when the heart of the fathers will be turned toward their children and vice versa. It will be one of the earth's greatest moments when children and parents begin to express appreciation for one another.

Now does this mean that criticism has no place in the child-parent relationship? Of course not. Many of us have had extremely damaging parenting in our lives. It's wrong for us to remain susceptible to that kind of victimization. Positive boundaries are necessary. Biblical criticism that points out sin and error must be faced.

The key to criticizing in close relationships is setting a budget for it. Expression of thanks can be seen as the depositing end of parenting or leading. Each one of us has a different threshold for receiving criticism. A great critic is patient and understands that there are healthy doses of criticism and unhealthy ones. A critic who impacts lives for a lifetime will learn to judge the amount of criticism that brings true growth in his or her students.

Wanting to Be Wanted

Women often believe that men can withstand any blow to their egos. I find just the opposite is true. Every man craves to be accepted—not only by his wife but also by his family. It's a tough old world out there, and it's important for a man to feel respect and love at home. It's anything but heaven when a man finds his way home to a nest of mean criticism.

A wise wife who criticizes with the aim of making the listener feel loved and accepted brings real change. It's often said, "Behind every great man is a great woman." Actually the truth here is much more mysterious. Behind a good marriage are two people who know how to give criticism in a way that fills the other with courage.

Women crave their husbands' understanding. Any criticism a man brings has to be given in a manner that the sense of commitment is more evident than the criticism.

Men also crave understanding and tend to critique women in ways that work for them—so they can damage the women they love without knowing it. The Bible encourages husbands to relate to the women in their lives with great sensitivity. The apostle Peter even said insensitive or harshness in a husband can cause their prayers to go unheard.

Criticism in the family is the most delicate of all human communication. The emotional dependency that exists in a family can cause even a whisper to sound like a Super Bowl crowd. Two simple rules of thumb for all family communication are:

1. Does the listener feel understood?
2. Does the listener feel accepted?

What Should Be Criticized

Every family needs a game plan for correction. If we don't live deliberately, we'll live accidentally. And living accidentally is like planting a garden and never pulling the weeds. Paul's talk in Romans about the carnal man is an expression of a man or woman living accidentally. If we don't deliberately set out with a game plan for living in our families, unwholesome methods appear.

The first step in a family's strategy of correction involves knowing what needs criticized and what doesn't. Let's outline what should be criticized in a family:

1. Lapses in character such as lying or manipulation.
2. Any behavior that puts the family or individual in jeopardy on any level.
3. Behavior that is discourteous or thoughtless toward others.
4. Behavior that is destructive of other people's property.
5. Words and activities that tear down another person emotionally.
6. Behavior that hurts or damages another's reputation.
7. Behavior that sexualizes any relationship outside marriage.
8. Any attitude that shows disrespect for authorities or the elderly.

A clear game plan within a family should be set up to assure these issues will be corrected with deliberation. Now let's outline infractions that should be criticized very carefully:

1. Behavior that's simply annoying.
2. Correction focused on styles of dress.

3. Ineffective efforts in sports or other extracurricular activities.
4. Choices of practice, talents, or school majors.
5. Matters based on comparisons.
6. Opinions given in haste without thoughtful preparation.
7. Excessive weight gain or physical abnormality.
8. Accusatory comments about depression or other emotional problems.

A game plan for reproof is as important as making certain the family has a balanced diet. A solid approach to encouraging growth is one of the rare gifts a family can give to one another. Families can learn to promote success without smothering the gifts each member possesses.

Many of us share a blended family experience, which is much more complex than that of a nuclear family. The new parents must face the challenge of earning the right to criticize in these complex relationships. Sometimes it's best that the plan be developed by the parents and gradually introduced into the home. Nonetheless, great care must be taken to pinpoint and govern the amount of criticism in a family. Again, don't forget that ten thank-yous for every criticism makes for a happy family!

How to Be Heard

The aim of criticism, as we've seen, is not ventilation but helping others actually grow, to express love in a growing home. Love is primarily seen in the effort to listen. It's a law of human communication that if you listen you'll be heard. All communication must begin with knowing others as well as possible.

If a parent or spouse wants to be heard, the best way to begin is to ask questions, such as "This is what I've observed—is it true?" "Would you mind if I mentioned a topic that might be sensitive?" "Did you really mean to leave the garbage on the dining room floor?" "Did you really call the neighbor a moron?" Allow the disciplined one to explain or correct your perceptions before landing an assault.

Questions show a desire to understand and make certain that the facts are straight. Seeking to view things from another's viewpoint is also a necessary step in showing respect. We all respond much more positively to correction if we're allowed to participate in the adjudication.

Below you will find a diagram of the four necessary ingredients of a healthy critic. I encourage you to take some time and consider your last few criticisms of others. See if you need improvement in any of the four facets of spurring others on.

The Four Pillars of Biblical Communication

Intelligibility	Empathy
Credibility	Neutralization of Fear

Intelligibility

Believe it or not, much reproof in a home goes unheeded because the listener doesn't understand what's being said. The emotional force of the comments can blur the message. Or the exhortations may be overheard by a child.

My son used to play little league basketball when he was a young tyke. I hardly missed a practice or game. One of the fathers was the coach of the team. He had the habit of blurting out harsh instructions not only to the whole team but also specifically to his own son. His methods embarrassed everyone but no one more than his son. I don't know how the boy survived some of the verbal attacks. I suspect they may be paying for counseling these days.

Some of this man's tirades included three different and conflicting instructions. They would range from "Surge ahead—get that ball!" to "No, do it delicately—be careful!" to "Back off, back off—you're getting too close!" Now these are all good instructions, but when they come within three or four seconds of each other, the message is unintelligible.

I've learned to ask people I counsel to repeat back to me what they think I said. I spent years assuming it was the other person's responsibility to understand clearly what I was saying. And even when giving admonition for work poorly done, I have learned to ask the person to write down what he or she thinks I said. Once I know we both understand my complaint, then we can progress to the cure.

It's important to remember that all life-giving correction is a democratic event. All parties must be part of the outcome. Again, you need to be concerned about this part of communication only if you're looking for positive growth. If you just want to ventilate and don't care about growth, then blast away, and never mind the understanding part.

Empathy

Empathy is the ability to look at someone's struggles from his or her perspective. Recently I was in a discussion as a consultant with a church about their tremendously low staff morale. I have in the past been the *cause* of low morale, so you could say I know both sides of the fence. In my past leadership experience I know I was gripped too much by time pressures and overcommitment myself, and this caused me to be very insensitive when things didn't go right.

I have improved over the years by coming to see that Jesus sums up the Law and the Prophets with this beautiful statement: "Do to others what you would have them do to you" (Matt. 7:12). So in a nutshell, if you're going to criticize others, criticize in the way that you would like to be criticized. I know for me that this means I want to be criticized very little. But second, I really want to feel the other person cares about me personally.

Empathy is the most difficult of all human skills. It's one of the chief indicators of emotional maturity. Empathy also runs a fine razor's edge to unhealthy enabling. Enabling means the willingness to accept any wrong behavior in order to keep the peace. This vital skill allows all conversation to be carried by grace and hope for the future. Empathy also avoids the pride trap that critics can take on in their corrections.

Anyone can listen to an empathetic voice. Anyone who makes the effort to understand another's pain will get a ready ear for his or her own complaints.

Credibility

No humans are fully credible at any time. Nor are any fully trustworthy all of the time. It took me years to learn this truth. I lived in a black-and-white world where I was either absolutely wonderful or you were totally wrong. A trusted friend helps me see that credibility comes in degrees, not black-and-white forms. I learned that, in fact, we're all a mishmash of good and bad. But credibility is earned when we look like our proclamations. It means that we approximate our message closely enough that the other can understand us by our actions as well as our words.

Forgiveness is a vital part of credibility. And repentance is also part of earning credibility. The person who admits his or her own weaknesses and makes a reasonable effort to correct the wrongs will always get a ready ear when he or she admonishes another. Don't be confused—the one putting on airs of perfection rarely gets heard. Any listener knows that there are no perfect people, particularly their critics. Someone who tries to bring correction from the mountaintop will never be listened to. Credibility comes from having walked through the trenches and come through as an overcomer.

And there is no environment that can compete with the family as being the most sensitive to hypocrisy. Our willingness to ask forgiveness from our children and family increases our credibility. And, of course, efforts to look like your speeches are essential as well in order to be heard while giving a rebuff.

I've had to work at overcoming many faults. I've found that far from turning people off as a leader, my willingness to exhibit growth has allowed me the platform to help many people. Repentance or self-deprecation, however, means nothing without visible steps to improve. Progress raises credibility sufficiently to be heard.

Neutralization of Fear

Nothing stops communication faster than fear of rejection. I can't listen to anybody if I fear he or she will reject me when I tell the truth.

A great teacher learns to hear his or her own fears and silences them. And truly effective guides learn to anticipate the fear in their listeners before they speak.

Denial is always symptomatic of fear. People deny their wrongs, their addictions, and their sins because they fear punishment. Denial is usually followed by anger in wrongdoers. Anger is a sure sign you've hit a fear when giving correction. I've seen some angry explosions in my office as a pastor, some by children exacerbated by criticism. Others were unleashed from husbands threatened by their wives' criticism. I learned over time that all these responses to criticism were driven by fear. My role as a pastor or counselor is to render fear powerless in those I seek to help.

John the apostle in his first epistle taught us that love casts out all fear (1 John 4:18). Anyone who communicates a life-giving reproof must become skillful at neutralizing fears such as the fear of rejection. Fears that affect one's health include the fear of embarrassment, the fear of looking stupid, and the fear of punishment.

Parents and spouses—and as far as that goes, anyone—must take the time to show that fears are unwarranted. It may seem encumbering, but anticipating each of these fears before bringing criticism will definitely increase the likelihood of a great family.

The Worst Criticism

Silent indifference is the most painful criticism in any family. I opened this chapter with a memory of Jack and Jill, who had fought and argued bitterly with one another. Let me now mention another couple, Jim and Joyce. They owned and ran a business selling vacuum cleaners, sewing machines, and the like. I had met them through a mutual friend, and they began attending our church.

I visited their business to buy a vacuum cleaner some months after we met, and you could cut the tension with a knife. So I wasn't surprised when several years later they came to see me about their marriage. They wanted to end it but were in conflict about their children. Their fault-finding with one another had escalated to the point that they had become silent critics. They both knew the other was disappointed but no longer even attempted to express their unhappiness. Both had been hurt by the other so many times that they just stopped talking.

This long period of silence in itself was a criticism of the other. Basically, this kind of criticism says, "You're so unworthy of my words. And I'm not even going to make the effort to communicate." Most every couple goes through periods of this kind of silent treatment. It's a power play at its very core. Silent criticism kills any relationship. And it grows to be the manifestation of pure hate.

This kind of criticism must be replaced by biblical criticism to save a troubled home. The Bible guides us toward loving interaction with one another that confronts pain and wrongdoings with truthful words. Silence must move beyond its subtle power to forgiveness, and then forgiveness must move on to listening. Listening must progress into the loving desire to change for a rich home life to develop.

Actions do speak louder than words when all has been said and done. And breaking the silence is the greatest of all healing actions. No healthy relationship can exist in silence for long.

Jim and Joyce made it through their threshold. All three of us studied Matthew 18 and other passages that refer to speaking the truth. They worked through layer after layer of disappointments in one another and a couple of sins until eventually there were only the day's sins left to talk about. They agreed that they would never again use silence as a punishment but that they would as quickly as possible express their criticisms of one another.

Adrenaline and Low Blood Sugars

Joe and Linda attended the second church I led. Not only were they high-energy people but also they had both come from highly argumentative families. Their home had evolved into one in which you had to be pretty hardy to survive.

However, theirs was a very loving home at the same time. Their children adored them. But they had almost daily bouts of unusually destructive criticism. Joe came to me first, seeking help.

"Pastor, our home is horrid," he said. "There's none of Christ's peace. We fight and yell constantly. We want help."

I met with them several times. I'm not a trained professional counselor, so I took great care in counseling them. Most of us pastors are trained to give spiritual counsel, but when it gets to some of these situations, we rapidly need to get outside help or make a referral.

I contacted a friend of mine who was a psychologist in Colorado on behalf of Joe and Linda. I told her I had this couple who was strong spiritually and clearly loved each other but that almost every evening they had knock-down-drag-out fights. These fights were usually preceded by some criticism one had toward the other or the children.

I reported some of the conflicts were over such small things as bicycles left in the driveway, a mop turned upside down in the closet, or a failure to get the telephone messages off the answering machine. I said all of these were probably annoying but that they were amplified to the point of becoming reasons for World War III in this family.

Dorothy responded with one question: "Are they fighting before dinner?"

I said, "I think so."

She said, "Well, here's what you tell them to do. They need to stop and get some energy drink or eat a Snickers bar on their way home and agree to not try and communicate with one another until they've eaten. What's happening is that their blood sugars are so low, they can't stand a lot of dissonant communication. And criticism can sound like dissonant communication."

I was excited to meet with Joe and Linda for our next appointment. We began our counseling session with prayer, and then I asked what had happened the last week. Predictably, just by my bringing the situation into the light, I learned that their explosions had dropped down to three or four a week, but they said they were certain they would escalate at any moment.

I related to them the advice I had gotten from Dorothy. They both said it made sense. We agreed that we would get back together within three weeks and assess Dorothy's strategy. Sure enough, this strategy led to an abatement of the intense and destructive blowups. They learned to be intelligent about their communication and continued to work on breaking the bad habits they had learned in their childhoods. Criticism moved from the idea of being a foe to that of being a friend.

Medical aspects of a person's life can affect criticism. Such things as a malfunctioning thyroid, diabetes, depression, and even immune system difficulties can make one hypersensitive to criticism. And he or she can turn into a cranky person.

Couples Who Criticize Well

I've always admired one of my friends who is a missionary now home on furlough. He and his wife have a remarkable marriage. I've always wished I had the skills that they have in communicating with one another. It's a delight to watch someone who's good in relationships. Relationships never come easy for me. I'm more of a quiet, self-contained, and observant person. I've gotten better over the years at engaging with others, but its hard work. I've suffered a great deal of pain because of my inability to understand the intricacies of communication. But that may be why I've sought to learn all I can about the sort of communication we're talking about in this book.

Mike and Susan, my missionary friends, have one of the friendliest relationships I've ever seen. I've noted, in my observations of their marriage, nine traits I see in healthy marriages that increase their quality. Why don't you take a look through them and see how they apply to your life?

1. Whenever there's a need for criticism, either to give or receive it, they make it fun. They laugh with each other after the intensity drops.
2. They never demean or make the other feel small.
3. They're constantly affirming one another in love.
4. They put everything on the table. Neither of them is the type who buries complaints or hurts, and they never use silence as a tool.
5. They refrain from calling each other names. I've spent a great deal of time with them, and their respect for one another even when angry has amazed me.
6. All of their communication is laced with words of commitment.
7. Their complaints are very specific and never general. Never do they say "You always . . ." or "You almost never . . ."

8. They have the confidence to leave the topic if the other doesn't receive it.

9. They do get angry at one another but know when to back off until both are prepared to deal with an issue with wisdom.

★ ★ ★ ★ ★

All these traits apply to the wide range of communication experiences in our lives. I encourage you to consider the material in this chapter and make it a part of your life. Let's close this chapter with some questions to think about.

Can you think of a present need to criticize another?

Can you take a moment and consider what he or she might fear in your admonishment?

Have you been the recipient of any name-calling? How did it make you feel?

Is there a person who has criticized you without hearing your side of the story? Can you build a desire to avoid this kind of criticism yourself?

Criticism in the Marketplace

W E LIVE IN a thrilling time of advancing technology and productivity. However, these advancements are a double-edged sword. The shock of constant change is causing nerves to rattle, and our emotions look for scapegoats for our stress. One of the deep, dark truths of the American workplace is that criticism is shrinking productivity. Without a turnaround, this human foible could undermine the health of the marketplace.

Business leaders have told me that criticism from newer and younger employees aimed at the older leaders in organizations is freezing the effectiveness of many businesses. The criticism is moving far beyond ideas for improvement offered via the suggestion box. The situation finds business leaders deliberating how to take this negative energy and turn it to helpful criticism. The task is difficult, because our communication skills lag far behind our ability to innovate.

The generation of the Vietnam War decided they were never again going to be caught in the grips of a dead-end business or organization. Their anthem of "Question all authority" in their youth has shifted to "Question everyone in the marketplace" in their adulthood.

A case can be made for the need for fearless analysis. The new culture of criticism has enhanced the drive for analysis and has resulted in some very positive innovation.

Of course, one of the tradeoffs for an innovative workforce is a great deal more questioning of the status quo. Business needs to discover systems that curtail pointless criticism and yet allow for the creative flow of new ideas. But in the meantime, criticism has gotten out of hand in the marketplace. The culture of Jesus offers a powerful cure for this challenge.

Store Owner

Recently during a lunch break at a seminar I was leading, I complained to a bunch of businesspeople about staffing issues in churches. Everyone seemed interested in the few things I had learned by speaking with personnel experts. I have never been great at personnel selection or issues, so I wanted to learn all I could from experts in order to better help churches and myself.

As I complained about insubordination on church staffs, one of the businessmen began to chuckle. Jerry owns a chain store that sells videotapes and was in the process of buying up three or four more locations that week. He had been a successful high-end manager for one of North America's best companies for twenty years. But his life dream was to own a small business.

He spoke up after my little speech and said, "You preachers just whine, whine, whine. You ought to try leading a workforce in the marketplace as a Christian. And the worst employees seem to be Christians who feel they can question me because they know God too. You have no idea what it's like to try to train a group of young adults on how to keep records on video stock. And it's an even bigger job teaching the new recruits how to apply rules for ordering new stock. They rarely follow what I've trained them to do. In fact, every instruction I give goes through the filter of each employee's preference of how they would like to do it. They follow their preference and forget my instructions. The longest I can get my best employees to follow instructions is a month."

He paused and then continued: "I even had one employee recently criticize the fact that I didn't show up on weekends, so why should they have to work weekends as well? I just wasn't ready for that kind of comment. When I grew up, the boss was the boss. Not today. You're open for criticism even though you're writing out the paychecks."

I started laughing along with the other five members of our small circle. I said, "Do you have any more insights for us, Jerry?"

He said, "Yes—we need some help as Christian businessmen on how to apply biblical principles in that kind of situation. I'd just fire them all, but the problem is that when I fired some for insubordination or tainting the work environment with criticism, their replacements were just as bad. I think this excessive evaluation of authority is epidemic everywhere. The marketplace needs help as much as the church."

I didn't advise businesspeople in our church as much as I could have over the eighteen years that I pastored them. I wish I had spent more time with businesspeople trying to find answers to the real challenges they face. I wish I had spent more time reading, as I've been able to do the last few years, on business challenges. Businesspeople more than ever want to bring the Bible into their world.

Fortunately, I've had the opportunity to invest in gaining ideas to help business build an environment that thrives. My role as a speaker in many churches is allowing me to teach positive ideas in the marketplace and the church. I think many of these applications of Scripture could help businesses led by Christians become healthy centers of powerful business creativity.

Expect and Normalize Criticism

Negative evaluation in the marketplace can be curbed in any business by employing the following insights:

- Jesus taught his followers that criticism needs to be formal and structured, not ad hoc. Formalized systems of feedback render unhealthy criticism powerless. It's amazing, but encouraging formalized criticism as a part of the workplace and guiding it positively can reduce criticism in the marketplace. A good deal of negative backbiting in businesses is due to the lack of positive outlets for complaints. A monthly feedback sheet from a workplace team asking how they can improve operations can gain a lot of good will.

- Systematically rewarding new ideas that get implemented is another way to focus critical energy in a business. When a business rewards ideas for change, tearing down other people becomes less attractive.

- Criticism can become helpful if problems are bravely discussed even if emotions run high. I've often found that when churches have a great deal of conflict, a good "steam-letting" session can bring back a constructive environment for growth. There's nothing like clearing up months of misunderstandings and healing hurt feelings to restore productivity.

- A business or organization can experience only what it chooses to reward or confront. Criticism becomes helpful when there is an enforceable and enforced protocol for criticism. The most important portion of a company's protocol is the promise of demotion for triangular communication.

★ ★ ★ ★ ★

Jesus Christ warned us of the dangers of triangulated communication. It's essential that all criticism be given to the person in question. The person who is not producing or is hurting the environment must be confronted one-on-one. Ill-intended accusations or belly-aching in organizations must be dealt with swiftly. If you enforce correct evaluation and celebrate when it's done properly, your organization will flourish.

Preemployment training on how disagreements are handled in your business could save a lot of headaches. I can't remember having this kind of protocol ever explained to me in jobs I've held. And all too often I had to face an environment filled with back-biting and false accusations. If there is an absence of a process for handling criticism effectively, the void will be filled by harmful patterns of communication. Most places I have worked didn't bother to confront divisive employees who were nearly scuttling the business. I would have enjoyed my work a great deal more had there been preemployment outlines of how criticism would be presented.

Effective businesses take great effort to reward positive, optimistic people in their workforce. If fear begins to rise in an organization, things get very toxic. A leader's optimism allows employees to move beyond their fears.

Optimism in a company diminishes the critic's influence. There are plenty of examples of leaders whose optimism created powerful companies, like Sam Walton, Bill Gates, Jack Welch, and others who are clearly optimistic people. These kinds of leaders see setbacks as an advantage to create a new productive future.

An admirable skill many leaders possess is that of leaving toxic issues in the past. If criticism is forced to face a visionary and positive leader, it loses much of its power. The corporate culture that can move on and remember that finding out who is wrong has never really solved a problem will win over its competitors. If a culture can make the future a friend, unwanted evaluation in the workforce will decline.

Spit It Out before It Eats You Up

I help coach a little league baseball team for kids with a parent who was legendary as a highly competitive coach. My son signed up to play, and I agreed to help the little guys as a coach and umpire. I like to win, but not as much as this man did.

It was frightening how important winning was to this man. He was highly emotional and childish in attempts to stomp the competition, using silence to manipulate the kids in directions he wanted. He brought in his people skills from his business, a friend told me. If a player wasn't performing up to his standards, he would look away, shake his head, and turn silently into the dugout. If he pulled a kid from the game, he offered no encouragement—just silence. This is toxic criticism at its worst.

Silence leaves the recipient perplexed, wondering what he or she has done. Employees need to clearly hear from management. The silent treatment will erode any organization, as it will a home. Disrespect for the coach was the price our team paid. Great business has brave leaders that are able to confront with good news or bad news. If the rank and file need to be criticized, then do it boldly—but never punitively. This is the Jesus way of handling conflict in the business sector.

Three Types of Criticism in the Marketplace

Restorative Criticism	Punitive Criticism	Instructive Criticism

Every piece of criticism should be planned carefully in any company. Choosing the form of criticism you use could determine your bottom line. If an employee were to train his or her managers to assess which type of criticism they were bringing into the market, criticism could indeed become a friend.

Restorative Criticism: This is criticism designed to bring relationships back together while confronting a real problem. Restorative correction is intended to move everyone into the future with greater hope and vision.

Punitive Criticism: Punitive criticism is focused on who's wrong and how he or she should be punished. This method doesn't contribute to the long-term success of an organization. Criticism that seeks to put someone in his or her place will spread negative attitudes through an organization like the flu.

Instructive Criticism: Instructive criticism operates off the premise that everyone in the company wants to do his or her best. Criticism aimed at giving new skills to work develops a thriving culture with great camaraderie. This kind of criticism asks, *How can I help replace the bad behavior I have noted with new skills?* This view sees the criticism as only part of a total training experience.

Criticism and Gossip in the Marketplace

Gossip is thievery. It is criticism that steals another's reputation, and it's forcefully rejected in the Scriptures. I've always been fascinated by the way that the book of Revelation lists gossip as one of the terminal sins of humanity. Over the years I've come to understand why God so hates gossip. Gossip is a felony against all that's godly. It takes something from its target that can never be brought back— a person's reputation.

One day I had a conversation with a member of our church leadership team about gossip and criticism in his business. He said, "The worst people who have worked for me so far are Christians. I avoid Christian kids [he hired a lot of people from the age of eighteen to twenty-five] like the plague."

Naturally, I was surprised and asked, "Why? Aren't they better workers?"

"Sometimes—when they want to be," he replied.

"Could you explain that to me further?" I asked.

"Yeah. For some reason these Christian kids, knowing I'm a Christian too, all feel they become spokespersons for the Lord. They're the most gossiping workers I've had and the most critical of me behind my back. They come in late and wonder why I'm upset. I've concluded that the church world is a lot like a bad family sometimes, or it could be thought of as a poorly run army. I've never seen people so ready to create a tainted work environment in my life than a group of young Christians."

"So what have you done about it?"

Bill said, "I try to hire people who are just raw pagans from other businesses with good work records and pay them well. I think Christians might think that since they're Christians the Christian boss is obligated to keep them on board."

"You don't make any attempt to confront or speak to any of these kids about this at all?" I asked.

"No, I really don't have time, Doug."

I pondered this conversation for quite a long time. I rehearsed it with a fair number of businesspeople, and they all had the same response: The criticism of Christians in the workplace negatively affects their bottom line, and the pleasantness of the work environment was jeopardized. This sloppy living often undermines their influence as God seekers.

As leaders, we have not taught the importance of character, the avoidance of gossip, and the straight talk that's needed to combat gossip. I've also wondered if problem employees' expectations of their boss aren't what drive their disappointment. Bill was a visible leader of the church, and I wondered if his position possibly caused employees to view his Christian kindness as a big temptation to take advantage of him in the business.

How to Give a Biblical Reprimand in the Marketplace

I was never trained to be a boss in my preparation for ministry. I did for a period serve on a moderately large staff, where I learned a host of bad habits as a boss. I cringe sometimes with the way I handled conflict in my early days as a senior pastor. I had little idea how to go about confrontation with the long view in mind.

I wish we leaders could start out with twenty years of experience—then we would have little place for the fears that distort our guidance of others. The fear of doing things wrong, the fear of the consequences of bad decisions, the fear of rejection, the fear of not having enough—all these were extremely prevalent in my life. Most people in leadership face these same fears but rarely recognize their influence on how we criticize others.

Eventually I found part-time staff and myself leading a church of 150 members. I was ill equipped for the challenge. I made some significant progress on how to inspire a workforce—but, like most churches, there was not enough money, not enough time, and usually not enough personnel to get the job done. These shortages caused fear and tension. If I had to do it all over again, I would do things I learned in the later years of my ministry. It takes pretty rigorous training to learn how to bring bad news in a healing way to a staff.

I would never give a reprimand unless I took the time to write up my thoughts. I would also review which kind of criticism I was about to give. And I would never again buy into the lie that if we could identify the violators in our team, things would go better. Things go better only when solutions are sought and rewarded. And I would never give a written reprimand that wasn't based on clear expectations and a job description.

Since leading my own church, I've worked with hundreds of churches as a consultant. I've taken time to interview some great bosses and have sought time with personnel experts asking them what makes for a healthy work environment. I've also had the opportunity to work in the marketplace outside church work as a consultant. Over and over I find that the power of healthy reprimand is the glue that keeps a workforce producing at peak levels. And on the reverse side I've come to be frightened of the negative power of destructive criticism.

Steps for Giving a Proper Reprimand

A written reprimand should be given with the following steps:

1. It should include a review of the contract's specific expectations. The unmet expectations should be factually confronted and discussed.
2. It should have a clear set of steps to take to assure improvement. This could include a clear line of training to cover deficiencies.
3. It should include a reasonable time line for improvement.
4. It should include a new contract outlining expected improvement from the date of criticism.
5. It should outline an objective reporting process. This process of close review should include a schedule for several midterm evaluations before the period of probation is over.

The Best Kind of Reprimand

Self-criticism is always the most biblical kind of criticism. It is the most mature pathway to full development. A manager who can train a staff to be self-reprimanding will make things hum in his or her business.

This kind of approach instills growth from the inside out. And such organizations create heroes. So often I've seen students raised in Christian homes enter the marketplace or a secular college and fly apart morally and academically due to a lack of inward discipline. I've had many high school and college instructors tell me they can easily spot a student raised in a strict Christian home, that he or she often has very little self-discipline. The best and most successful students grow in situations in which self-evaluation is encouraged and modeled.

Capricious Bosses

One of my staff team says, "If I could just know what was important to you, I could do a better job." His job was constructing our strategic plan, which was to include a plan for funding and developing systems to prepare for our growth. I'm a highly creative person, some say, and like many creative people, I can miss the importance of spelling out expectations. The future is a very friendly thing to me, because I'm a visionary. Details can get lost with creative types. And we can look capricious to systematic people.

Many great leaders by nature are not great managers. Usually they're caught in the big picture more than in the immediate management of systems. They tend to inspire rather than to direct and are therefore sometimes fearful of the details of organization.

A friend told me he thought that I was a little capricious. I didn't agree with him at first, but with further thought I saw that I had let workers down by not making expectations clear in ways they could easily understand.

I actually am vitally strategic in my approach to work. I follow straight-line logic, but I plan far ahead and have multiple backup scenarios.

I suppose even my team today would say, "It is really tough to get Doug to spell out instructions." And this isn't good. But we're all learning to hold criticism until we've learned to present expectations in ways our learning styles adapt to best.

Most people like clear progress. People want rewards, and they also want to hear when things aren't right. But they require a great deal of stability to embrace criticism that impacts their employment. Succeeding in the marketplace simply breaks down to doing to others as you would have them do to you.

How to Criticize

W E HAVE STUDIED the nature of toxic and healthy critics. Now we will outline actual step-by-step processes to do effective criticism. Knowing how to apply new ideas is the crown jewel of education.

One of the best ways to learn anything is by contrasting two different ideas. I'm sure you remember grade school nicknames. I had a friend we called "Skinny." He wasn't skinny, though—he was actually heavy. (We used studies in contrast to define him better.) Skinny didn't seem to mind it any more than he liked being called "Carrottop."

So first we're going to play the devil's advocate by defining what would be the opposite of healthy confrontation. Let's try to apply this with a new angle we've all learned. And who knows? Some of you may want to become a destructive critic, and now you'll know how to pull it off. Smile!!

How to Execute Criticism Poorly

1. Jumping to conclusions is a perfect way to make mistakes with your criticism. Many people believe they can know another person's true motives without so much as a conversation. I've known people who can meet someone and figure out their sins within ten minutes. This is why all criticism must be preceded by questions. A sound critic stops to ask the question "What is it I don't know in this situation?"

2. Failing to ask for clarification is also another oversight that can cause your criticism to miss the mark. I know a couple who interrupt each other constantly and don't even notice it most of the time. I've seen one of them make a misstatement that caught the attention of the spouse. When the spouse tries to correct the errant comment, the other will pounce on the spouse. The conflict escalates, going back and forth through several stages that are too complicated to note here. Communication is mainly the give-and-take of words. Words are just codes that seek to transmit a picture in one's mind to another. This process is a very complicated one. Good communication is something like an Olympic sport that requires intense training. Clarification is part of good communication. A good critic always asks to clarify things from the other's point of view before drawing conclusions or criticizing.

3. Joining forces with others who have been offended by a person is an effective way not only to be heard but also to create far more serious problems in a group or organization. This malpractice is an art form the church world has perfected. If offended by a pastor or another person in the church, a person can cause more damage by seeking out others who feel as he or she does. I've found this kind of accusation procedure can be predictive, because it will always

bring the worst behavior out of the confronted. It will turn a nice guy into a monster overnight. Yes, if you want to be a destroyer in your church, collect all the offenses you can on all the people you can, and form an army of critics to put them in their place. You'll be certain to cause irreparable damage to relationships and your church.

4. If you develop a style of confronting that requires the buildup of lots of agitation and anger, you can set new records of harm in relationships. Adrenaline is a powerful fuel, which is never helpful in relationships. If you fear another's reaction to your criticism, it's likely you'll be ready to pounce at the first sign of negative reactions on his or her part. It's best to not confront anyone you fear.

5. Accomplished heart crushers always trust their emotions above fact. I wish I had a dollar for every time I heard someone say in the midst of conflict, "Well, I just feel that I'm right." It doesn't really matter how you feel most of the time. Your emotions are loaded with influences from your past, present, or fears of the future. And these stored-up wounds can explode without notice and tear relationships apart. Your emotions must be subservient to the protocol of Christ and the substance of fact.

6. If you use threats in your criticism, you can turn a small problem into a feud filled with retaliatory actions. One of my favorite quasi-spiritual comments goes something like this: "We feel that if you don't straighten out the pride in your life, Pastor, God is going to take your ministry from you." I've heard this statement directed at a pastor friend by one of his board members. We must remember that God never threatens. He does give us warnings, but these warnings are far from threats. Warnings remind us of consequences that we will face with continued wrong behavior. Threats, on the other hand, set up an adversarial relationship.

7. Overstatement is another terrific way to turn criticism into confusion. Statements that start with "You always" or "You never" can inject a person with shame as you criticize him or her. Overstatement is unproductive because it just isn't true. Healthful criticism is based solely on the truth. Overstatement turns people into caricatures. I hate it when people use over-statements with me. Tell me that I was rude to you yesterday on the phone by not listening closely to your instructions. But please don't tell me I "never" listen to you. That just isn't true—I listen at least 20 percent of the time. (That was a joke.)

8. Speaking for God is a great way to taint your criticism. A statement like "God told me to tell you that you're a miser-able flop" is an immature way of saying, "I'm irritated with you." I feel sorry for God sometimes because of the way he gets credited as the source for the irritations of critics. Personally, if someone can't show me a scriptural reference for his or her criticism, I don't pay any attention to the cor-rection. I'm frightened by people who believe they know what God is saying to everyone else. The good news for all us victims is that God is not a gossip.

9. Loving conditionally is reliably destructive in any relation-ship. If you withhold affection from your child until he or she gets perfect grades, you'll be certain to take your child's motive for succeeding in life. Conditional love feeds feelings of loneliness and rejection. Criticism without unconditional love hardens hearts. It never facilitates growth.

Positive Ideas

Let's flip the focus now to positive steps to offering healthy criticism.

1. Healthy criticism matches the complaint with the style of the listener. Seeking to understand what drives the person

you're criticizing gives him or her enough security to consider the correction carefully.

2. Healthful critics are able to pause and put themselves in the recipient's shoes before criticizing. They ask, "How would I feel if I were receiving this criticism?"

3. Real helpers remember that no one remains the same for long. Criticism is a response to a moment in the learner's life. I've been told that every marriage over its lifetime actually evolves through five marriages wrapped up into one. Most people grow through some mighty impressive thresholds as they stick close to God. We're always more than what we do wrong. And healthful critics never leave someone frozen in time in his or her worst moments.

4. Friendly criticism is preceded by an encouragement for every criticism.

5. Solid criticism expresses the value and importance to the other person.

6. Healthful critics see forgiveness as the natural conclusion to criticism. This is exactly what Jesus did for the Samaritan woman. He confronted her and then offered God's forgiveness. This act of forgiveness soon spread to a whole community of Samaritans. All believers are priests authorized to offer forgiveness from God.

7. A biblical critic is committed to helping the listener move beyond the wrongs. Biblical help comes with a willingness to sacrifice and to lend help to the criticized. I've had the privilege as a pastor of helping many substance abusers on their way to healing. I've found that one of the greatest things I can do for a friend is to attend an AA meeting with him for his first time. It's not enough to simply criticize his addiction.

8. Healthful critics maintain their loyalty to the individual when they confront. I've caught myself at my worst, enjoying making another feel rejected when I had to confront

him or her. I would collapse with agony if I didn't know that all of us from time to time like making others feel rejected. Rejection kills hope and peace. Anytime you criticize another, there needs to be commensurate statements of loyalty.

9. Sound criticism considers the other person's emotional state. There are times when none of us can take anymore criticism. If someone, for example, has just lost their business, they really don't need a lecture on doing a better job hiring personnel. A poor emotional state doesn't put most of us in the mindset of the learner. Healthy friends measure the person's state before they begin criticizing.

10. Effective criticism is handled briefly. Nothing is more agonizing than a long rebuke. Biblical criticism sticks to the facts and gets over it quickly and moves on.

11. Healthy critics speak for themselves, not others. It's never healthy to quote other opinions of the person you're confronting. Making statements like "The rest of us on the board all feel the same. I'm not sure I agree with all of them, but they all feel that your sermons are getting too long" create fear, not healing. If you're on a church board, for example, and feel that the services of your church are going too long, go to the pastor and say, "I think the services are going too long," and leave it at that. Resist the temptation to collect statements from others confirming your concerns. Everyone will be better off if you do.

12. Great critics leave the response to their criticism up to the listener. A sound critic understands that our role isn't to manage the responses. Rather, it's to speak the truth in love and trust God and the one criticized with the responsibility of his or her response.

13. Sound critics don't assume they know the pain in another's life. I was trained as a grief counselor to never say, "I know

exactly how you feel." I made the mistake once of telling a mother who had just lost a son, "I know exactly how you feel." This middle-aged mother's eyes lit up like fire. She sternly looked me in the eye and said, "Pastor, you could have no idea of how I feel right now." I had to acknowledge that she was right. Speak only for yourself. Maybe even confess, "I don't really know what you're facing with your life, and I couldn't even begin to try to guess."

14. Welcomed critics are able to keep confidences. Usually when people fail, they need a confessor. And it's hard to find a worthwhile person to confess to. Critics who are welcomed find that speaking the truth in love can elicit confessions from their friends. Toxic critics spread what they learn in the confidences of others. Healthy critics gain credibility because they give the listener reason to trust that the details of their sins and faults are held in confidence.

★ ★ ★ ★ ★

I recommend handing the preceding list to leaders and managers who are in a position to correct. I have given it to many churches, and their morale over a period of time has soared. Many churches have been transformed through this same material presented in seminar form. This has confirmed my belief that churches are filled with very wonderful people and that problems arise because we simply lack the training and skills needed to help one another. It's great for a church group when they learn to express their irritations and pain to others in a way that helps.

All communication has eternal qualities. Good communication is more valuable than gold. It's a myth that some naturally communicate easier than others—communication is such a complex process that it takes deliberate effort for everyone. Yes, it requires disciplined effort and thoughtful preparation every day. Accidental communication will usually turn sour right before your eyes. Communicating well is a strategic act. And that's why this list is so helpful.

Can you think of any occasion in your family or work when you've done more harm than good? Do you find you tend to treat people closest to you with less respect than strangers? Do you find that your criticism is ill timed and seems to cause more problems than help? If you answered yes to the above assessment, I recommend you hang the preceding list above your desk, shaving mirror, or nightstand.

Can you think of circumstances over the last few weeks in which you've made someone feel good about being criticized? Can you note where others have gained greater courage from your correction? Have you received thanks for criticism you've given with statements like "Thank you—that was the perfect thing for me right now" or "This was a hard process, but I'm glad we went through it?" If so, hooray for you. You're on your way to sharing healing gifts.

Looking in the Mirror

If others have to point out my faults, I know I haven't been living a deliberate life. Somewhere along the line I had missed self-evaluation. It's advisable that you take time to consider how it is you could harm others and not be aware of it. Can you learn to face life better with what you've learned from being confronted? Self-evaluation requires a great deal of courage on a regular basis. It can be frightening to look into the mirror of your own behavior. Spiritual advisors try to encourage us all to regularly assess our sins and unloving acts.

Now this doesn't mean you should become a guilt-ridden person. A friend who was driving me to school one day stopped three-quarters of the way through an intersection because he noticed that the light had turned red. His tires squealed as we slid to a stop. He backed up halfway through the intersection and waited for the light to turn green. Several pedestrians were humored by the antic. Of course, the drivers behind us were horrified.

I asked my friend, "Do you ever have a problem with excessive guilt?"

He replied, "I just know God requires from me the best I can put out."

"You know, it's perfectly OK to not notice a red light and go carefully through the intersection," I said. "Your abrupt stop was more dangerous than going ahead on through it."

Self-evaluation should revolve around the question "Are my actions hurting or helping others? Are my actions honoring God or dishonoring God?" But never should we end up with the conclusion that we're helpless or without value. I encourage you to take a sheet of paper, draw a line down the middle, and on one side list hurtful behaviors you've expressed toward others. In the other column list healing actions you've taken that have helped others. And then use your personal assessment as a tool for your own "becoming."

Hurtful Behaviors	Healing Actions

Now try another exercise. Take another sheet of paper and place this heading on the left side: "Things I've done that have dishonored

God." On the other side compose a comparable list under the heading "Things I've done that have honored God."

It's impossible to live significantly before God without living deliberately. Human relationships are challenging enough without the collisions of living accidentally.

Sound relationships require the help of the Holy Spirit. The fruit of the Spirit does not consist of targets or goals; rather, they're simply signs of the presence of God's love in one's life. They're the manifestation of a deliberate relationship with the Holy Spirit in every moment of our lives. The fruit of the Spirit, however, never just fills our lives. These traits, which Paul lists in Galatians 5, are the result of a deliberate relationship with the Holy Spirit.

Many people I know seek to grow spiritually with passivity. They refer to this as living in grace. They wait but without being available. The Holy Spirit is no friend to laziness. Real grace occurs when we understand that our empowerment for life comes from above us, upon us, and within us. And we have no ability within ourselves to please God without living close to Him.

Hurtful criticism most of the time is the result of laziness. It does take work to communicate well. And possessing the character to give guidance to others requires the influence of God to be effective.

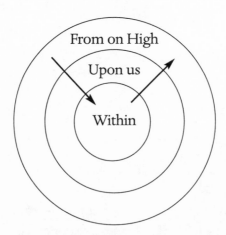

Deliberate surrender is the call of the Christian. Deliberate praying brings us nearer to God. Deliberate contemplation releases God's power. C. S. Lewis said, "Heaven understands hell and hell does not understand heaven. . . . To project ourselves into a wicked character we have only to stop doing something and something we are already tired of doing, to project ourselves into a good one, we have to do what we cannot and do what we are not" (quoted in Elisabeth Elliot, *Discipline: The Glad Surrender* [Old Tappan, N.J.: Fleming H. Revell Co., 1960], 62).

Observation confirms that no one by nature without the Holy Spirit's influence can be a healthy critic. And no one living accidentally is invited again to criticize.

Seeking Feedback before Giving Feedback

An important exercise is the discipline of asking for feedback from others. I know of a psychologist who after three sessions asks his patients to fill out a feedback sheet. He states, "This isn't the day when experts can speak from on high and bring much healing."

He said, "I noticed in my training for my Ph.D. that there was an air of inapproachability that began to progressively come over students who at one time were fairly decent counselors. I find that self-evaluation and evaluation by patients is something that isn't done very often. We were encouraged to have mentors or fellow counselors who would give evaluation from our files and the kind of care we're giving others, and the maintenance of our own emotional health. The patients were rarely invited to be copartners in their care, and I think this is part of the healing process. There are very few people who just want to be criticized or nodded at in a session; they want to feel that they are clearly understood."

The doctor is right. We live in a day when people are much more aware of themselves than they used to be. I think medicine has also realized that unless a patient shares in the knowledge of his or her diagnosis and prescription, the treatments don't work as well.

I've never yet seen a board of a church ask for an evaluation from the pastor or the congregation. Even boards, when left unevaluated, can become hindrances in churches. Anyone who leads should be open to feedback. This is part of the deliberate growth that assures us authority when we lead God's work.

I recently got a call from a church leader who said, "Doug, I've been asked to take on a church in Arizona that's had some trouble. The pastor prior to the one who just resigned was immoral and tore the church up. The second pastor lasted only two years. I feel a little nervous about signing on. I have all the hard data, but I'm concerned about the intangibles. You know me—I need your input."

I replied, "You know I've worked for several years at a prevention plan for pastoral sexual misconduct for boards, pastors, and denominations to use to face this epidemic. But recently I've also noticed critical boards that hold back way too many churches in fear. I suggest you ask all the board members to report on their giving and their commitment to Christ, plus ask them to take an emotional health test and maybe a personality profile of every member as well. Then do the same with staff."

"Are you kidding?" he asked.

"No, I'm not," I replied. "If a church isn't evaluated, then the church develops an environment much like one between a parole officer and a parolee. One-sided criticism or praise is not the pattern for healthy churches.

The following cycle leads to healthy encouraging and confronting. I encourage you to take some time to visualize this process working in your own life.

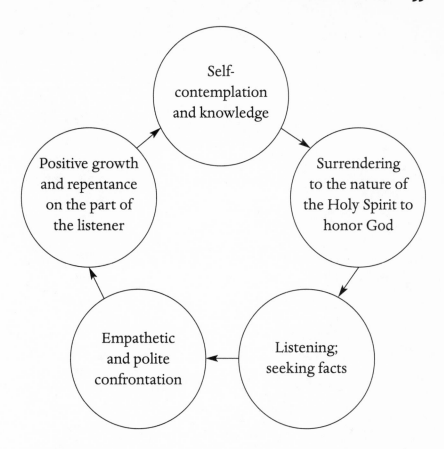

Great influencers are very deliberate about their criticism. Learning to be methodic and conscientious about confronting others can make life easier for you. And the quality of your correcting others will assure that you receive the same.

CHAPTER

Criticism in the Church

THE NEW TESTAMENT reveals a church under the scrutiny of the Holy Spirit. The apostle Paul told one of his favorite churches, the church at

> It seemed good to the Holy Spirit and to us.
>
> ACTS 15:28

Ephesus, to take care that they didn't offend the Holy Spirit, that he was their vital link to God. The Holy Spirit is the voice of God's correction. It's impossible to manage life's journey without his guidance.

The prophet Isaiah told his congregation that in the days ahead of them they would hear a voice of guidance behind them, pointing out the way. Jesus promised that the voice of God would guide his disciples if they had "ears to hear."

The prophetic ministries in the early church included Spirit-directed criticism. Paul spent two chapters (13, 14) in his first letter to the Corinthians on how such ministries were to be carried out. The Holy Spirit is very precise in the tone and intent of the correction he taught them.

Susan was a Christian who had been influenced by radical charismatic Christians. She often had "words" from the Holy Spirit to give our congregation. I usually was able to politely handle her enthusiasm. I knew she honestly wanted to share thoughts that would benefit the church.

Many times she would pull me aside after the service and say something like "The Lord is telling me that the church doesn't love enough." Another time the insight might be "The Lord is telling me that your speaking is too loving—it needs to be more direct." And yet on other occasions it might be something like "I feel the Lord is saying that the people up front are getting too egotistical." There seemed to be no end to her ability to spot danger within the church. I had grown appropriately skeptical about this kind of help over the years, but I tried to remain kind.

I decided that though Susan secretly drove me crazy, there could well be someone who might have a criticism we would want to hear. The Holy Spirit, I know, will not leave his church uncomforted.

Does God Gossip?

Does the Lord gossip to people in a church about others? I don't think so. The Bible says the church should be on alert anytime there are two or three witnesses who distinctly bring the same insights or reprimands.

I learned over the years as a pastor to recognize at least the process of listening to legitimate adjustments to the congregation. I am not sure that I always discern perfectly the sound of the Holy Spirit's criticism. It is vital to learn how to receive and test a correction given in the name of the Holy Spirit. Of course, the pockets of people who sit around and discuss unmet agendas or preferences in our churches fall into the category of unwholesome critics. The words of these people should be rendered powerless in any church.

However, it's important to remember that a church may need to have witnesses within pointing out problems that need correction. The early church thrived when its ears were open to the Holy Spirit's voice.

What Should Be Criticized, Praised, or Ignored in Your Church?

Most of us don't know what should be criticized, let alone how to go about it, in our churches. All of us could use a regular refresher course on what's best left uncorrected. What should be and what should not be left alone? Are there things we need to be praising before we criticize? I think the answer to the latter question is *yes!* Let's take a look at some praiseworthy actions.

What Should Be Praised?

1. Hard work should be praised and valued. Paul informed Timothy in 1 Timothy 5 that those who labor hard in the Word and in leadership should be paid well.
2. Generosity must be recognized. Acts 4 tells about a man named Barnabas being praised for his generosity to the church. His name means "encourager." His generosity doubtless encouraged the whole church.
3. Mentoring or sharing insights with others is to be praised, according to Paul.
4. Winning the lost also requires praise in a church.
5. Faithfulness is an attribute to be praised as well. Leaders who are faithful to their call and faithful to the church and others are to be praised and thanked for their efforts.
6. Showing honorable character under pressure is another praiseworthy act every church should be thankful for.

138 CRITICISM: FRIEND OR FOE?

Kindness and consideration should be traits that receive a badge of honor as well. There are, of course, a great many other aspects of church experience in which praise might be worthy—the list above is a very limited sample. Imagine the changes that might occur in a church if half of every board was given the assignment of organizing praise reports and celebration for the church.

One of the roles I have now as an itinerate leader and consultant to churches often places me in a critical position. But most churches hear far too much of what's wrong with them. So I've adjusted my primary energies in the direction of pointing out what they're doing right. Most churches are languishing under self-criticism or the criticism of the negative peripheral people who plague every church. Some forget that the Holy Spirit had a good bit of positive things to say to the church through his prophets.

The final book in the Bible contains a letter to seven churches whom Jesus loved and led (see pages 140–141). He begins most conversations with the churches with things they're doing right.

If someone fancies himself or herself knowledgeable enough to speak out about any church problem, he or she should be required to list twice as many things that are right as wrong. And second, the person should be willing to have his or her own life audited.

I have the important task from time to time of helping churches find pastors. Recently I helped a Southern church find a pastor with experience in "seeker sensitive" ministry. They put the man through about three personality and work-style tests, and they contacted about twenty references we had given them. I thought this was a necessary process, having gone through the process myself on three occasions. The church didn't know this guy and all the research that can be done on leaders. But when the process was over, the candidate said, "OK—I want the whole board to take the same tests I've taken, and I want an honest survey of each member's spiritual history. I also want some references on the staff."

It was one of the most momentous meetings I have been in throughout thirty years of ministry. I thought a couple of the board members were going to faint. My friend, the pastoral candidate, went on—"I don't want to lead a group of leaders who just do evaluation of me and don't want to submit to the same processes. It's not authentic leadership."

I didn't think they would accept him as their leader. Two of the members nearly quit, but I think just due to peer pressure they went along. There's a beautiful culture that develops from mutual accountability, which I saw there. I think Ronald Reagan's chant to the Russians of "Trust but verify" fit here.

A bit later, I visited the church when I was in that city to speak at another church. I met with the pastor after their service.

I asked, "How are things going?"

He said, "I knew even you were taken aback by my request for the board to be scrutinized just as I was. But I'm so glad I came into the church on these terms. We're really a solid group now. And we all know we're under scrutiny of one another and the Holy Spirit. There are no board of directors or employee pastors—we're all leaders seeking to honor God."

I know as a church leader I've had many authentic critics in my life. I've learned quickly to tell the difference between cranks and legitimate witnesses to church life. One of the chief signs of a God-endorsed critic is that they celebrate what's right in the congregation. But no leader can afford to wince at the process of knowing how to listen to a critic. A church that has developed a strong God esteem can hear adjustments because there's hope and trust to know God can be in criticisms from the church.

Church	Praise	Confrontation
Ephesus	• They do hard work and they hang in to the end. • They cannot tolerate hypocrites in their midst. • They test the claims of leaders.	• They've abandoned their first love.
Smyrna	• They've held up under hard times. • They're smiling even though poor. • They've held up under the attack of Jewish antagonists.	None
Pergamum	• They haven't compromised under great pressure.	• They've allowed corrupt leaders to remain in place.
Thyatira	• They have shown great love, faith, service, and "hanging in there" qualities.	• They tolerate a woman teaching falsehood. • They tolerate the mixture of pagan sexuality with their church.

Church	Praise	Confrontation
Sardis	None	• They aren't who they appear to be. • They've lost their first commitment.
Philadelphia	• They've kept God's Word under great resistance.	None
Laodicea	None	• They're lukewarm. • They rely on worldly riches as indicators of spirituality. • They've forgotten how in need of Christ they are.

What Should Critics Ignore?

The following is a list of issues that often get a lot of attention that would be best ignored in church life, or at least not get a lengthy platform.

1. A church member's own preferences for how things should be done.
2. Criticism of what has already been corrected and repented of.
3. Criticism built on the words from unknown second and third parties.
4. Criticism pointed at simple human behavior. (Sometimes leaders are depressed, overworked, and easily come apart

at the seams; these moments of human frailty are occasions to love.)

Regarding the last item, I've recently encountered a series of churches with pastors who have experienced long periods of depression. This kind of depression causes many unknowing human traits to come through. The sufferer is usually unaware that he or she is irritable or even caustic. Several of the pastors I've encountered have even become paranoid, feeling people are against them; they're unable to focus and express a lack of hope for the future. These are seasons in a church's life when grace is essential and everyone needs to step back and look at the big picture. The only pertinent question at such times is "What's important to us?"

It would be truly a wonderful world if members of congregations would learn how to spot pastors or other leaders experiencing depression or other human difficulties and illnesses—ignoring their emotional crimes and seriously addressing the problem. A murmur of complaints in a church at this time isn't helpful. Strategic ignoring and then offering help can be extremely healing in these situations.

I experienced a season of criticism myself by leaders and non-leaders in my last pastorate. I speak of it easily because I felt God even used that to lead me to grow into a better person. It was decided that I had too many ups and downs, and people were concerned about me. The root of the problem, which we found later, was a malfunctioning pituitary gland. I had medical issues I was facing, and it affected my moods. But many well-intentioned people decided I had spiritual problems. In fact I did, because physical illness can cause spiritual problems and vice versa. I survived just fine, but I experienced firsthand the church's inability to see their leaders as humans with human challenges.

These kinds of issues should be met with patience and encountered with love. Certainly, they should be addressed with directness. But criticism based on a lack of knowledge can be deadly to a church. We need a great deal more intelligence about how we handle such issues. All causes for behavior should be analyzed before conclusions are made.

What Are Prophets?

In the Old Testament, prophets were those who held Israel accountable as the people chosen by God. They were professional critics who in a sense were the conscience of God's people. These spokespersons carried out at least two functions in the New Testament:

- Forth-telling
- Foretelling

The forth-telling function brought both encouragement and correction to the people—hope for the future in the truest sense.

How do we know who the prophets are today? I've thought about this long and hard as a leader. I've seen many come and go who thought they spoke prophetically to the church. I've sought to learn how to spot legitimate consciences of the church. Here are some tests in evaluating would-be "God-given critics" to the church:

1. Are they open to criticism themselves?
2. Are they active, viable, and giving to the church?
3. Do they perceive themselves as part of the problem?
4. Do they offer specific solutions?
5. Are they willing to be tested and wait to see if others agree with them?
6. Can their concerns be confirmed in the Scriptures?
7. Are their confrontations based on specific details?
8. Are they willing to be anonymous?

I've found my little checklist to be very effective in allowing me to spot truly designated spokespersons. As I have said earlier, no church can afford to go without evaluation. It isn't just leaders either who need evaluation. Often it can be a church member in need of evaluation or even the attitudes of an entire congregation.

I encourage any harsh critic to remember that most people are pretty beaten down already. And in my experience as a consultant, I'm even more persuaded of a prevalent brokenness in families and even Christians today. Most congregations need a friend to point out what they're doing right. However, there's also a time to point out specific needs for improvement with humility and the sensitivity of a surgeon.

The spirit of authentic prophets must always be consistent with the nature of the Holy Spirit. We find in the Scriptures very clear help in understanding the nature of the Holy Spirit. The following results ring through when someone is being influenced by him:

- The Holy Spirit always makes clear his unconditional love for the church. We always see an explosion of joy when the Holy Spirit's truth is shared.
- The Holy Spirit always exalts the role of Christ on earth as Savior.
- The Holy Spirit always speaks with two or three confirming voices or experiences.
- The Holy Spirit is without respect for persons. In other words, he's willing to tell everybody the same thing. Would-be critics too often have prideful spirits that believe they're the only ones the Holy Spirit is talking to.
- The Holy Spirit never leaves fear in the trail of his work.
- The Holy Spirit causes people to look forward with empowerment to move on to greater and larger things.
- The Holy Spirit craves to send the awareness of forgiveness.
- The Holy Spirit is concerned with holiness. He seeks to make us all his sheep and like Jesus in our behavior.

- The Holy Spirit only knows the dialect of the Scriptures. He always illuminates the Bible while changing behavior.

I've valued this checklist as a guide that keeps me from being influenced by groundless critics. It also keeps me grounded in giving a wise response to what I feel is wrong in another's behavior.

The Danger of Hidden Expectations

A great deal of criticism from the rank and file in churches is the result of unspoken expectations about what the church should be. I wish I had a nickel for every person who attended churches I have led who joined the church with the intention of changing us into their image. These are invalid critics. And sadly, such critics are in ample supply throughout our churches. They seek to make their new congregation in the image of the best they've experienced in the last several churches they've been a part of. It's just plain wrong to operate this way.

A reasonable exercise in qualifying a person's criticism is to get the person to write down what he or she expected from the staff member or church he or she is criticizing. In fact, I encourage you to do this here as you read this book. If you have concerns about your church, why don't you make a list of the things you expect? Then make another list by interviewing one of the leaders of the church about what he or she perceives the church is to accomplish and how. It could be that your frustration with your church simply stems from the fact that you're in the wrong place. And you may have hidden expectations that you're not aware of that are making it difficult for you to become a part of the community.

A high level of intolerance and consumer-like "shopping" is going on in churches today. That's really too bad, and it's unlikely the church will change to fit the shoppers' liking. I've found that the best reason to be part of a church is that you're called there. One way to know if you're a fit is the "I'm at home" feeling.

The next test is to ask if you're needed, then to ask if you support the cause-and-share goals of the congregation. If you don't take seriously steps to ascertain these facets of your church membership, you'll soon become an invalid critic. Hidden expectations are never a valid basis for demanding change on another's part. And they shouldn't be the basis of accusing a church either.

Love, Acceptance, and Forgiveness

Perfectionism is a terrible aim for any church. The reason is obvious—the day will never come when everything is done perfectly in a church. But any church can be healthy, and that requires the presence of three major ingredients: love, acceptance, and forgiveness.

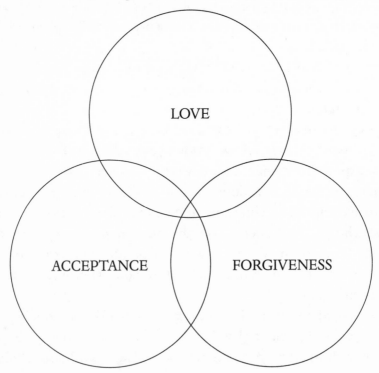

Again, forgiveness means the discipline to avoid identifying people only by what they've done wrong. Acceptance does not mean approval, but it does mean that we embrace others with full knowledge of their starting point and accept them where they are. Love was identified by Jesus as doing to others as you would have them do to you. A group that masters these elements of community will bring healing even in the midst of criticism.

The Holy Spirit does the transforming. A community skilled at loving, accepting, and forgiving will see the Holy Spirit do tremendous miracles in their midst.

One of the dearest friends I've had over the years is a well-known rabbi who is the leader and director of a ministry called "A Fellowship of Christians and Jews." He's given his life to helping Christians and Jews understand one another.

I asked him one day if he was uneasy hanging out with an evangelist like me. I further said, "Doesn't it make you nervous that I could get an awful lot of points for converting a rabbi to Christianity?"

He responded, "No not at all. After all, doesn't your New Testament say you're to love and that if there's any converting to do, that will be up to the Holy Spirit?"

I quipped, "How am I doing?"

He replied, "I'm still a friend of yours, aren't I?"

Stopping Toxic Critics

Toxic critics in the church must be stopped. In nearly every one of Paul's epistles, he took aim on them and discredited their influence in churches. A toxic critic is someone who doesn't align with the traits of the Holy Spirit we outlined earlier and whose aim is simply self-aggrandizement or imposing their preferences.

I'm shocked by how often evil critics in churches go unchecked. A number of years ago I was called to give counsel to a pastor who had suffered great agony in having to leave a church as a staff member. He called and asked what to do when another staff member (in the church he had been fired from) asked to meet him and then repented for deliberately defaming him with his previous employer. This staff member confessed that he had made up accusations about my friend in order to advance himself.

This kind of criticism clearly falls within the category of evil. I encouraged my friend not only to forgive the person but also to insist that this staff member make restitution even though his sinful act had taken place six years earlier. I told my friend to encourage this staff member to write a letter to the board and former pastor. This staff member's letter should ask for forgiveness while using this occasion to clear my friend's reputation. If the staff member refused to write this letter, then at that point, my friend should chose to overlook the sin and move on.

In my church consultation ministry I've also encountered board members who were opposed to the selection of the church's pastor. So once the pastor was placed, they would watch and spot faults at every turn. Their aim was not to improve the church—it was to get their way. Pastors' families and entire congregations are permanently harmed by these toxic critics.

What should happen to this type of critic? He or she should be given the left hand of fellowship and asked to leave a church unless he or she repents and shows a change of behavior. We're quick to confront many categories of sin in the church, yet the evil expression of vicious criticism often receives credence from denominational leaders, board members, and unwitting church members. We have often accepted evil as normal.

Someone who repeatedly brings conflict to the church should not be allowed to have any influence. I've suggested that chronically critical board members hand in their resignations and cease to be part of the church. Yet on the other hand, a church can never afford to discourage criticism that follows protocol in the true spirit of Christ.

The sins of gossip and false accusation must be seen as more injurious than sins like alcohol abuse. These types of individuals must be stopped even if it means significant loss of income to the church. There's just too much harm being done to churches by such people.

Nine Ways to Tell the Truth Healthily

Sometimes well-meaning people become toxic. Part of the leadership training we need in order to be analytical and to limit criticism to that which keeps the church on track should include the following checklist that describes legitimate criticism, correction, and truth telling.

- Legitimate criticism is always shared first face-to-face with the person in question.
- Legitimate criticism is never based on secondhand information.
- Legitimate criticism must be very clear and specific. Beating around the bush causes all kinds of problems when it comes time to correct.
- Correction brings wanted change when it aims to see a positive outcome.
- If the correction is rejected, effective critics objectively analyze their own hearts.
- Truth tellers must have the creation of harmony as their objective.
- Truth tellers must first evaluate and assess ideas; they then address specific behaviors.
- Truth tellers must offer a hand to help.
- Truth tellers must be able to release the outcome to God.

Public Admonition

In both of his epistles to Timothy, his youthful understudy, Paul asserts strongly the higher accountability of leaders in the church.

Leaders are to give great effort to watch for even appearances of wrong. A life of constant scrutiny is the life of leadership.

Paul also asserted that if a leader sins, he or she is to be admonished publicly. Paul's aim here was that the admonishment of a leader could result in a renewed commitment to right on the part of the church.

This kind of direction was not designed to take place in a church's Sunday morning services. Why? Because, essentially, in these services we're having "guests over for dinner." They include too many visitors and broken people for this kind of correction. In my home we never discuss issues pertinent to our family with guests in our house. It's understood that there are things discussed in a home that never go outside the home. This should be the way of the church. A church should save these events for a special meeting or membership meeting.

I recently spoke to a wonderful church in a Canadian city. The congregation had suffered great difficulty with an assistant pastor there. He had been released of his duties due to his immorality yet was offered the opportunity of being restored as part of the church. This initial infraction was handled delicately, and the information was contained within the leadership. I felt this step was biblical and would help bring healing. The pastor was bold and honest in the way he approached the problem. As is usual in these types of situations, the pastor was the object of criticism from those who spoke openly about the former assistant's sins. And the former assistant was in a position in which he could not really defend himself. But the correction was made, and forgiveness was offered. Thinking these situations can have a win-win end often trips up church people. These and other situations usually cannot get beyond the lose-lose level for everyone.

The pastor invited those who were part of the congregation to remain after the morning service. We had coffee and some refreshments while the church band played some background music. After about ten minutes of mingling, the pastor called us all together. He proceeded to inform the church that his previous assistant would not be allowed to be part of the church. He outlined some of the pertinent details of the situation. Then came a question-and-answer time followed by a prayer time for the previous pastor and his family.

The spirit in this meeting was, of course, loaded with agony and pain, but also present was a sense of great hope for the individual's family. And there were prayers of restoration for all concerned.

Criticism has an important place in the church. But it must be handled with great care. A review of this chapter would be well worth your while. I have no doubt that a church's health and effectiveness will rise and fall on this one issue.

How Does Jesus Criticize?

FTER A VISIT to the Soviet Union and observing the persecuted church (before the fall of Communism), I decided that the North American church behaved more like a utopian sect. Utopian sects seek perfection on earth. Christians in North America often see Christianity as a pathway to no financial problems, no discomfort, no disappointment, no struggle. But God never made this promise to us.

I believe a lot of criticism is hurled in churches because members seek a perfect world, and then harsh criticism turns on those who disrupt the making of a perfect society. The Bible clearly describes the church as a community empowered to thrive in spite of its weakness and to impact an imperfect world. This kind of reality requires deliberate preparation to face human imperfection.

I'm amused at how surprised we are when humans fail. All of us are bound to do some pretty stupid things in our lives. Thus, we need a plan to handle wrong and sin when they come—this plan is called protocol. We should expect the worst to happen and have a system of protocol for handling it. Embracing reality in this way will allow us not to be victimized by sin but to be a positive force to overcome wrong when it appears.

Speaking your mind to others is a challenging business. It's like doing relational surgery. Jesus gave his church a process and stringent protocol for giving criticism. Following this protocol is the vital process to joy and peace in any church.

This protocol calls for studious action. We shouldn't forget that correct confrontation is something we're incapable of without God. Jesus taught us to consider how we would feel if we were on the receiving end of what we're saying. And he also taught us to stop and consider the other person before we speak.

Emotional pain that is held internally will fester and become a root of bitterness that harms many. As stated previously, a wounded person will be tempted to collect an array of individuals who have likewise been wounded by the same person. And soon the momentum to attack as a group has a life of its own.

I consulted a church in California that had grown quickly to several hundred people. I had been asked to come and help bring peace to what had been a joyous fellowship for several years but had more recently experienced turmoil.

The chairman of the board told me on the phone, "Doug, things were going so well, but overnight things have turned bad."

"What started the trouble?" I asked.

He said, "Well, the pastor started living very high. He pushed the board to authorize the church to buy a huge house."

"And so they bought the house?" I queried. "Why didn't anyone speak the truth to him? It seems simple enough to me that a group could have said, 'Pastor, this extravagance is going to hurt the church.'"

"No, we didn't really know how to go about it," he thoughtfully responded. "Most people who were concerned just left the church."

"Well, let's set a time for me to come down. Does the pastor know you're talking to me first?"

"Yes, he's really broken up about this, and we all agreed we would help him through this process. We're losing some beautiful spiritual momentum right now because of all the criticism."

"OK—we're going to do a seminar for all the leaders on how to criticize Jesus' way. People do get outside the lines and need to be confronted. It's so sad that some Christians just leave at the first sign of trouble."

It took several sessions to develop systems for members of the congregation to bring helpful complaints to the leadership. The pattern Jesus gave us for criticizing wrong in the church saved this one. Now they're back on target and doing well.

Family criticism also requires protocol, because in a family criticism can often pass for attacks. The closer our ties with people, the greater the temptation to treat without common courtesy. And we know that when a family goes to war, the wounds are much deeper and emotions run much higher than in any other environment. It isn't difficult to see why this is so. The familiarity family members have with one another can give many things to attack one another over.

Dysfunctional families create dysfunctional protocols for dealing with misbehavior in their homes. I've found that in most dysfunctional families of addicts or emotionally ill people, criticism is seen as a supreme act of betrayal. These families avoid facing issues with feelings of panic that the wrongs will be discovered. Dysfunctional homes are always concerned about appearances, and admitting wrong is just too close to the heart of life in the home.

The protocol that dysfunctional families follow first involves denial. Secrecy is also a component of the family's response to destructive behaviors. Passive hostility soon follows. The hostility comes from suppressed anger that eventually implodes within the angry victim.

The first step in correcting a dysfunctional family system is to acquire the boldness to begin confronting wrongs in a healthful way. Jesus' protocol for criticism works like an antibody clearing away the infections that have harmed the family.

Healthy efforts at correction don't require that all criticism be correct 100 percent of the time. After all, Jesus said in Matthew 18 that when you're harmed you're to go directly to the one who sinned against you, and you're to confront the person with regard to his or her harmful behavior. This first step is done obviously with care, because the accusation may not be right. If the accusations are found to be untrue, then that's the end of the story. Criticism given in this way is far better than internalized accusations.

Is It Necessary?

Criticism is never fun, even when proper protocol is followed. It's not supposed to be fun—it's supposed to be true and life-giving. The wonder of Jesus' pattern for criticism is the fact that it uses up so much less energy than criticism run wild.

Renowned English poet Samuel Taylor Coleridge wrote a poem in 1799 about his feelings for one of his critics. It's titled "To a Critic: Who extracted a passage from a poem without adding a word respecting the context and then derided it as unintelligible."

> *Most candid critic, what if I,*
> *By way of joke, pull out your eye,*
> *And holding up the fragment, cry,*
> *Ha! Ha! Those men such fools should be!*
> *Behold the shapeless dab!—*
> *And he who owned it, fancied it would see!*
> *The joke were mighty analytic,*
> *But should you like it, candid critic?*

In the eighth chapter of John the Pharisees threw a partially clad adulterous woman at Jesus' feet. John recollects for us that Jesus looked around at the crowd, knelt down, and wrote something in the dirt. We don't know what he wrote. But it must have been an indictment of the women's critics. After writing, he rose up and looked at the accusers, saying, "He that is without sin among you, let him first cast a stone at her" (John 8:7, KJV). The crowd first slowly and then rapidly dispersed. No one wanted to be a critic on Jesus' terms.

I think Jesus' point here was "Is this criticism really necessary?" Everyone there knew it wasn't authentic. This woman was being exposed so these fearful leaders could hide from the penetrating words of Jesus.

My friends tell me I behave more like a New Yorker than a West Coaster. I think I know what they mean by that. All my friends from New York are blunt, straightforward, and really care little if they're liked. I know there's often a meanness to blunt conversations, but sometimes I wonder if Jesus was as sold on "nice" as we are. I'm fascinated by the way West Coast communication entails as much effort to make it clear what you *don't* want to say as getting to the point you *do* want to make. This kind of environment leaves too much hidden that needs to be expressed. Likewise, the Christian community misses a great deal of God's intention by not lovingly telling the truth.

Respect and Criticism

Affirmation is part of the protocol of correction. In fact, one wise old businessman once told me, "If you want to have a productive workforce, you need to affirm and thank your employees three times as often as you criticize them." And he said he often asks himself these two questions: "Is the criticism I'm about to render even necessary?" and "What is the positive outcome I want to come from this confrontation?"

Respect is essential for expressing any bad news to someone. Respect means always remembering that a person is much more than what he or she does wrong. It also means being able to *differentiate* between the person and what he or she does. Protocol, when followed the way Jesus taught, reminds us that we're all created in God's image—and because of that, we're of inestimable value.

Formalized Concern

One of the churches I led had an extraordinary volunteer ministry. We rallied the assistance of 3,500 volunteers we called "unpaid staff." These people gave at least two to four hours a week in the care of the church. We found that to have a happy volunteer force, you couldn't just encourage and affirm—they wanted proper formal evaluation so they could know how well they were performing.

We had conducted employee reviews for years each quarter. We had checklists for their work attitudes, promptness, friendliness, recruiting, and completion of tasks. But it had never crossed my mind that formalized evaluation was vital to express respect for our volunteer force.

Silence rarely encourages anyone. I've proven that when a volunteer force isn't evaluated, it feels first unappreciated but also uncertain that they're performing well. Hard-nosed evaluation feels more like love to people than silent kindness.

As a church consultant, I've worked with hundreds of churches on how to build a happy workforce and have heard some very creative complaints about pastors. It isn't unusual in many churches to have five people on a ten-person board feel the pastor preaches too long while in a moment of confidential communication the other five say he's preaching too short. It's a no-win situation. If there are regular opportunities for feedback in formal ways, these kinds of concerns have the sap taken out of them, and if done properly, everyone learns—even the leader.

Jesus' kind of correction is never casual. The right kind of admonishment is formalized. In my last pastorate, we sent out questionnaires by which people evaluated various aspects of our church life. We asked them how they liked the topic I was speaking on and what they thought of my demeanor. Sometimes we asked questions about our services, such as whether the music was hitting the spot and adding to the message. Were there any needs for improvement in the ushering, the parking, or the building? We invited formalized criticism, because we felt we often received some fabulous ideas.

Let's go back to our volunteer force and how it worked. We designed a plan wherein one captain (a volunteer) would work with ten to twenty other volunteers closely. Part of this captain's job was to give evaluation and affirmation to the volunteers under his or her charge. It was interesting to observe that the sweeter-than-sweet captains had the least respect and most conflict from their areas of oversight. Those who applied formal evaluation were usually more appreciated and their workforce much happier with their ministry tasks.

I recall reading one captain's report to five small-group leaders under his charge. He had sat in on all their meetings and filled in a report based on a checklist he had prepared for each one. All of the five small-group leaders were clearly evaluated, and they loved it.

None of these small-group leaders felt put down, and no one felt emotionally assaulted. The assessments were based on predetermined expectations. Criticism that follows protocol holds its peace until the expectations are made clear and all agree upon the format for evaluation. And if the evaluations were missed, the lay leaders felt cheated out of a fulfilling part of their work.

This works well in homes too. I know one of the failings I made as a father was expecting things from my kids that I had not previously verbalized. I had never told them how their rooms should look. I assumed they knew what their mother and I expected. All healthful criticism must be preceded by an agreement between friends.

Private vs. Open Witness

Let's go back to Matthew 18. It seems to me that Christ was teaching us that sins committed against us in private are best handled in private. I think I can see why, since the hope of criticism is growth, not punishment. As stated previously, wrongs are better learned from than punished. When someone's sin or error is broadcast, usually the aim is to shame the violator rather than to improve lives.

Years ago I intervened in a situation in which a youth pastor had fallen into sexual immorality with one of the women in the church. I called in the assistance of a psychologist I knew in Colorado and asked her how she would recommend handling this challenging problem. She had some "counter-intuitive" input for me.

"Don't tell the whole church about it," she said, "but don't hide it."

I asked, "How do you not tell the whole church and *not* hide it?"

She said, "Obviously he's going to be terminated, and too often I see in churches that the reason it's announced is so the pastors and leaders won't be criticized for letting someone go. I feel that organizations today are too open about talking about this kind of sin.

"Our research shows that when these wrongs are announced publicly rather than helping stop the behavior, young people tend to get involved in sexual experimentation more than when things are handled differently.

"The extent of the public discussion should be equal to the scope of the sin. And proper protocol for a church leader should be to explain to the church in general how such things will be handled. The church can be prepared, then, to pray and save others the trauma of information that really isn't helpful anyway. And if the church has questions on an individual basis, part of the protocol should be providing a group of elders to whom the person can go and ask questions. And, of course, the individual who has committed the sins must agree to such divulging of information as well. It isn't a good idea to discuss someone's sins without his or her approval."

Her comments made a great deal of sense to me. A clear plan for dealing with human wrong limits the number of mistakes we make. If we take a case-by-case approach, we're susceptible to outside pressure and fears. Emotions run high at such times, and knowing how you'll handle sinful behavior by leaders beforehand can reduce the number of mistakes.

Jesus said the only time sin must be confronted in public is when someone denies his or her sin of wrongdoing. This cannot be determined until the person has been confronted. Should he or she be found innocent, Jesus said, it's OK that the question was asked, as we have seen. Such matters are to be brought before the church only when the person remains a danger, Jesus implied. The Jesus protocol makes provision for public warning if the person remains a danger as part of the community.

The apostle Paul spent some time criticizing the Corinthian church about their failure to remove a leader caught in sexual misconduct, more specifically, incest. And he said that because this person would not acknowledge his wrong, his practice was so threatening to the community that he could not be allowed to continue as part of the fellowship of believers.

Moving On

Forgiveness is always part of the Jesus protocol for confrontation but is often confused with approval. It can also be confused with decisions to ignore an issue and overlook it. Overlooking someone's error is just that—overlooking it. Forgiveness means believing there's more to a person's life than the moment of his or her error.

As I'm writing this book, the press has been filled with all kinds of agonizing betrayals. We've seen everything from 150 priests in Boston being involved in pedophilia to the recounting of the sins of a mother who killed all her children by drowning them in a bathtub.

Some fought for the woman's innocence based on alleged mental illness. I happen to agree that mental illnesses certainly can affect one's ability to make good decisions, but even in such situations there must be accountability for the behavior. There's a difference between understanding how a person behaves, having compassion on him or her, and overlooking his or her crimes.

I found myself praying for this young mother who drowned her children. I prayed that she would find the peace that comes from forgiveness. Excuses for wrong never bring peace. It's amazing how accepting responsibility for our behavior can make life so much more livable.

Forgiveness accepts explanations, but it never gives way to excuses. Genuine forgiveness can't be given until ownership of the wrong has taken place. But once we acknowledge our wrongs, forgiveness will disentangle us from guilt and sadness. Forgiveness seeks not just to neutralize but also to abolish the impact of wrong.

Forgiveness is love in action. More than that, it's allowing someone to move on no matter how deep the fall they take. It's the Christian's great act of liberation for all who do wrong.

The biblical pattern for correction calls us to anticipate how wonderfully we will forgive our listeners before we begin the criticism. The process isn't completed until we have given forgiveness.

Ask Questions

Our relationally impaired culture treats relationships with one common error—jumping to conclusions. We're horrid listeners in our society today. We have lots of noise but very little attentive listening. Jumping to conclusions is a symptom of wanting results without taking the time to know someone. Jumping to conclusions is a style of communication based on the well-known slogan "I already know what you've done—don't confuse me with the facts."

The kind of criticism Jesus shows up for requires there be an appropriate number of questions with which to test the accusation. The proper way to handle rumored wrong is to ask questions. These have to be *direct* to do any good. Far too often, Christians like to beat around the bush and speak in codes. We of all people should want to speak clearly and get it over with so we can move on to forgiveness and unconditional love.

I well remember an instance in my last church that still embarrasses me. We had quite a significant crew of both paid and unpaid janitorial teams. One member of the paid crew began to bother me. Every time I talked to him, he wouldn't answer. I thought he was shy at first. Then I became certain that he was rebellious. Next I even took it more personally and decided he didn't like me for some reason. Usually I was in a hurry when I gave instructions about a smudge on the wall or a coffee stain on the carpet and needed him to pay attention quickly. And nearly every time I tried to give him instructions, he tended to look away from me and not acknowledge what I said.

We met as managers twice a month. I spoke up in one of the meetings, saying, "You know that janitor with the glasses—what's his name?"

"His name's Larry," one of the managers said.

"OK—Larry needs to go. He never acknowledges my instructions. He never acts as if I'm talking to him—he just walks away. He's either recalcitrant, lazy, or both."

The room was as silent as if all the air had been vacuumed out of it. I mean deadly silent—like the quiet in a funeral home before a memorial service.

Finally the head of the janitorial crew spoke up. He said, "Doug, were you not aware that Larry's deaf?"

My heart fell to the floor. I now knew I had wrongly judged this individual for months in the worst way. I hadn't asked the right questions about him. I had broken biblical protocol and had nearly fired the man. I had jumped to conclusions about him that could not have been further off track.

Proper protocol in the home also requires not jumping to conclusions. No one but Jesus has ever read another person's mind. I tend to be very deadpan when I'm visiting churches, usually because I'm observing, as I've been hired to do, or I'm about ready to speak and am concentrating on my message for the service. Again and again I've had pastors ask me why I didn't like the service. They assume that my lackluster expression means disapproval.

I've tried to look enthusiastic, but I still look as though I'm not in the room. My wife thinks my demeanor is rude. But I can't help it—I concentrate in church. I've had to explain to many friends that you can't read my mind. You must ask questions before you judge another.

You can't judge motives either. If all of us leaders all got honest with ourselves, we would have to admit that we believe we can judge the motives of others. Media reporters judge the motives of our leaders, from the president to senators to many others. And I find a lot of hackneyed critics are good at improperly judging the motives of the people they observe.

Trust until Evidence Says Otherwise

Nothing is more harmful to relationships than distrust. I'm presently working with a church in the United States Southwest that's facing growth strain. The previous pastor served there for twenty-seven years and fell into unethical practices the last two years of his tenure. I'm not sure exactly what happened.

One of the leaders of the women's ministry in this church told me, "I don't believe the new pastor is trustworthy."

My reply was "And what do you base this distrust upon?"

She said, "I've been around his type before, and I can tell that he's not trustworthy."

Again I asked, "And what evidence do you have to support this?"

She said, "Just intuition."

I was getting a little hot under the collar, because I've been the target of such distrust without evidence. After I resigned from a church I was pastoring at one time, many tried to guess why. The reason for my resignation was my family and other ministry opportunities. I wanted to do what I'm doing now, which is evangelism. I'm also a church healer. Part of my assignment from God is to help churches heal so that they can be more effective at reaching people. I spent my first two years in the new ministry in my own hometown agonizing under rumors that I had either had an affair or had misappropriated funds or any number of other things—because no one could imagine a pastor wanting to leave a large church.

It stings when you're the target of irresponsible criticism. Proper protocol demands that we trust others until the evidence makes it necessary to do otherwise. Even when we find that a person is not trustworthy, our aim in confronting the person is to see him or her find his or her way back to trustworthiness.

Stick to Facts, Not Feelings

All our emotions are a mishmash of pain that has happened in our lives. That's why having protocol for criticizing is so extremely important. I was once on the staff of a church where an individual stole hundreds of thousands of dollars from the church. It was one of the most traumatic periods in my life. It was the first time I had ever had a job in a church, and I had fully trusted the person. I had trusted the pastor and the board to maintain protocol, and the church and I were betrayed. The experience left me cynical for years. This thief drove a yellow Cadillac and to this day when I see a yellow Cadillac with a mid-life to elderly person in it, I freeze.

We all have these kinds of emotional knee-jerk reactions in our lives. Protocol for criticism should call us away from such reactions back to the facts. Protocol protects us from the cynicism that affects our thinking from past hurts. We need help to avoid misinterpreting others.

Over the years, I have seen people ruined when Jesus' protocol wasn't followed. In one instance a young woman accused a youth pastor of seeking a romantic relationship with her. The elders in the church believed her. The pastor was happily married and had a stellar track record. The leaders had to listen to the accusation, but they never met with the youth pastor until they had made up their minds.

Several of the board members said, "Even an accusation such as this was reason for termination." Sadly, if they had taken the time to seek the facts, they would have found that this young woman had falsely accused three other pastors of the same thing. In fact, she went on to two other churches to do the same. The last of the churches had some intelligent leaders who investigated the claims thoroughly, including making calls to every church she had attended. They discovered a history of five falsely accused leaders she had ruined. They made certain she got help but also required she make restitution to those she hurt in order to remain in the church.

I want to finish this chapter with a quick review of the two kinds of protocol in bringing criticism. The first checklist is a description of dysfunctional patterns of dealing with bad news. The second is a checklist for Jesus' protocol.

Dysfunctional Protocol

Denial
　Anger
　　Comparisons
　　　Accusations
　　　　Rejection
　　　　Silence
　　　　　Hiding
　　　　　　Secrecy

Jesus' Protocol

Listening
　Prayer
　　Asking Questions
　　　Clear Confrontation
　　　　Forgiveness
　　　　　Offering Help
　　　　　　Encouraging
　　　　　Pray

The Restoring Community

W E'VE COME a long way in our discussions about criticism. We've learned, reviewed, and pondered pages of material—but there's more to come. This chapter is a review of the power of community found in the church's

> Brothers, if someone is caught in a sin, you who are spiritual should restore him gently. But watch yourself, or you also may be tempted.
>
> GALATIANS 6:1

criticism. The church's ultimate call to restore sinners to God is at the core of how the church treats people.

A few years ago I met a pastor in a city on the East Coast who had read one of my books and was interested in my concept of churches as healing communities. Jim began telling me his story and informed me that he was a recovering alcoholic. He had been a heavy drinker in college and had serious problems with alcohol even as a Christian before entering the ministry. He had been through rehab once and had conquered the addiction in his life for a number of years.

Jim hit some bumpy roads approximately ten years into the ministry. The stress of leading a growing church began to put pressure on him, and some bad habits began to reappear. He confided in me that he began to deal with the stress by having a little extra wine at dinner.

Then secretly behind his wife's back in his study in the evenings he began once again to have two glasses of wine, which grew to four, then six, which grew to returning to the hard liquor he had once been so fond of. No one noticed his growing addiction for a long time. He soon was hiding the bottles around the church. He was even drinking before sermons to calm his fears of not being liked.

His wife had never seen him during his addicted years, so the problem was growing right before her eyes without her seeing it. However, eventually she could smell the liquor on him and saw his behavior become more and more unpredictable. She didn't know what to do. She confronted him several times—but like many other addicts, he was able to talk his way out of it.

Jim began to choke up when he got to this point in his story. A member of the board of elders who was a psychologist contacted Jim's wife. He had detected the scent of alcohol on the pastor and had also noticed an increasing slur of speech during sermons. This doctor had spent his internship in a rehabilitation clinic treating alcoholics. He had also had enough training in alcoholism to know that it was a disease—and he knew Jim was in trouble.

The doctor and Jim's wife met with and informed the entire board of his renewed alcoholism. They all loved him and appreciated Jim's leadership. He had set the church on a course of strong success. But they knew this problem had to be faced, or they were all in jeopardy.

They scoured Jim's home for bottles and found several cases of wine and bottles of liquor stashed in various parts of the house. Then they searched his office at the church, and even in the ceiling they found bottles of alcohol he had hidden for use while at the church. They also found three or four bottles stuffed in his car. He had hidden all this extremely well.

Then one Sunday night after his evening service, the board called him together with his wife, and they began intervention. Jim related to me that the doctor on his board took charge of the intervention.

He knew he had been discovered as soon as he stepped into the room. They had placed several boxes of the bottles they had found, both empty and filled, on the office floor in front of his chair. His wife was crying as he entered the office. Also included in the meeting were Jim's oldest child and a couple of friends.

The doctor said, "Jim, you are our pastor—we love you, and we're committed to you. I understand that this is a disease that you have never completely defeated. We want you to get help, and we want you to get restored as our leader again."

The group laid out their plan. He would go to a rehabilitation facility for twenty-one days and then would go to a retreat clinic for pastoral leaders for another two months. Upon returning, he and his wife would go to a one-month retreat for couples. Then after six months if he were doing better, he would return to the pulpit and leadership of his church with the requisite that for three years the doctor would administer periodic urine analysis. The doctor put it this way, a variation of the famous words of Ronald Reagan: "We will trust, but we will verify."

The church covered his wages. In fact, several on the board covered most of it for the interim six-month period. It has now been six years since this traumatic event in his life and that of the church.

He said, "Admittedly it wasn't really great for the church initially. But we brought in an interim speaker, and my assistant began to do very well for the church. The church cared for my family. It seemed that many casual observers, rather than being turned off, were quite impressed with the loving way the church sought to restore me.

"Now the church is growing. I've come to see that it's not perfect people that church inquirers want to follow—it's imperfect people who have become overcomers."

Jim's story was similar in many respects to those of other pastors I have helped. Jim didn't stay at the church that restored him. He resigned after the first year because some of the coping mechanisms that had led him astray began to reappear.

Jim went on to serve as a college professor for three years and then joined a church staff as a pastoral care leader, which suited him more.

"If it hadn't been for my church loving me as they did and putting my restoration at such a high priority, I would have left Christ and despised my call," he said. "I've never been happier my whole life. And I have them to thank for that."

This story is a terrific example of confrontation in a church that was aimed at the high cause of restoration. We are called to be communities that give people back to themselves.

Heaven's Favorite Theme

Jeremiah the prophet is usually referred to as "the weeping prophet." I like to think of him as "the restoration prophet." In chapters 28–33 of the book bearing his name, he predicts the day when everything the nation of Judah had lost to the hands of Babylon would be restored to them. One of God's famous promises involves his "plans to give you hope and a future" (29:11). And again he said, "[I] will rebuild [you] as [you] were before" (33:7).

Judah had failed God miserably. Prophets for decades had pled with them to little avail. Even in the face of overt disobedience, God promised that they would turn and that he would restore them. Like all other prophets, Jeremiah looked forward to the coming of the Messiah, who would bring full restoration to God's people.

This message of restoration is at the core of Christ's work on the earth, and the Church's mission is to continue this mission of Christ.

Job's Unhelpful Friends

The book of Job is a remarkable story. It's generally believed to be the first written book of the Bible and deals with the age-old issue of why good people suffer. But it also deals with the restoration of all things. God's people are candidates for blessing, even though everyone may abandon us, our spouses may reject us, and our wealth and children may depart from us. God's intention is always to restore.

Three of Job's friends had explanation after explanation for his loss of wealth and family. They even chided him for the loss of his dignity, assuming that bad things don't happen to genuinely good people. They calculated for Job what God was trying to get at in his life. They missed the key fact the whole while that it was Job's righteousness that was far beyond their own that had gotten him into this predicament.

Job's life illustrates the great care that would-be correctors must take in admonishing others. We learn from this ancient story that not everyone who loses his or her reputation or wealth or even family is experiencing the consequences of his or her own sin. The story of Job settles the fact that this is not a "people-friendly" world. But God's presence is always there to revive and renew.

We learn from Job's unintelligent supporters that there are times when you should hold your corrections, step back, and watch for the restoration of God. The final verses of the book of Job are some of the most poignant in the Bible. We're informed as the book winds down that this faithful servant of God received a new family, and his riches and wealth were double what they had been before the losses. God lavishly restored to Job what had been taken—and more.

This is a theme that works in every believer's life, not just Job's. And if we seek to help someone with correction, we should remember that God's intention is always to restore what's been lost.

Word Pictures

The Bible is filled with inspiring word pictures. And the topic of restoration has no shortage of beautiful imagery either. Three particular Greek words are translated "restore" in the New Testament. Let's take a look at each of these:

The first word comes from a root meaning "to mend fishing nets." This word for restoration has its roots, as you might guess, in the fishing industry. Fishermen restore nets in the material sense, but God restores the broken nets in our lives. So when the community of restoration does its work well, we're mending nets that allow people to feel whole again. The final sense of the word is that when we are restored we're put back into full operational condition as we once were.

The second word means "to give back what was stolen." We've all been stripped of something by this world's thievery. Sometimes we've lost treasures we never knew we had. A restoring community helps us get back what was stolen from us through addictions, being victimized by our own stupidity. But God wants to give it all back to us just because he cares for us.

The final word means "to be fitted again." This word was a construction term, describing a brick mason's work when a rock fell out of a wall, involving the process of re-chipping and refitting another rock to replace the missing one. So in this sense the wall was restored to its original state.

Communities that heal help people by "refitting" them for success. We're called to restore people by helping to see the walls of their lives rebuilt by God. People who have lost their integrity need the community of restoration grievously. People today are broken enough that they often punish themselves plenty without our tearing them down. Admonition has to come with a willingness to bring grace into the picture, restoring dignity and health to an individual's life.

It's an awesome experience to be part of a church that loves, accepts, and forgives to the point that lives come back together. I've come to realize that this is the only way healing groups win their battles, by keeping in mind a healthy outcome in the way they deal with people. Communities that restore have never regarded a person as an imposition. These churches live to buy back what life has stolen from the lives of broken people.

I've found in helping addicts that nearly all addicts relapse at some point in their rehabilitation. I think for many years the church was the worst place for people coming off addictions. If an addict relapsed, we treated them as though they were no longer Christians. Just when they needed us most, we rejected them.

But now we know a great deal more about how addictions work. I train churches that seek to restore addicted people these days. There is an 85- to 90-percent chance that cocaine addicts will relapse within the first year. And nearly all alcoholics relapse at some point in the first few months or years of their recovery. We used to call this "backsliding." But it really isn't. It's the process every addict goes through, and they need the church to travel with them.

A Personal Story

I went through a series of losses over a period of several years. I resigned a large church because I wanted to help other churches and live a slower paced life. The shock of having to have a whole different work style, along with the loss of the familiarity of leading the same church for eighteen years, was nearly more than I could take.

My life then filled with a number of other shocking losses for the following two or three years. The first was one that might sound trivial to you but almost brought me to tears. Isn't it interesting how we can weather a series of large losses, and then along comes a small manageable one and we fold?

I had purchased an expensive soft lamb's leather black coat in Chicago. I loved this coat and wore it wherever I went. One of the first places I spoke when I began our Square One Ministries was Montreal. I love Montreal. It's truly a beautiful city. I had wonderful hosts when I visited, who showed me all of the quaint places around town. One of the stops I most enjoyed was a place where we were served pancakes with maple syrup coming right out of the tree into the boiling pans of the cooks.

On the second night of my stay in Montreal I decided I wanted to check out a downtown movie theater. While standing outside the Hilton Hotel waiting for a cab, I noticed a van filled with young people driving by me not once but twice. Then they appeared a third time and pulled up in front of me, sliding open the van door while still moving. Two young men got out of the van and walked toward me. One of them was holding a knife, which he put under my chin while the second young man said, "I want your coat."

My response was "I want you to have it." I handed it to them, and they drove off. I was a bit shaky for a minute, and after a few minutes of deep breathing, I went in and told the hotel clerk about the robbery. I continued my stay in Montreal and still have pleasant memories of the city—but I couldn't help missing my coat.

Now let's leap to July 2002 in Melbourne, Australia. I spoke to a congregation led by a pastor I had never met. I spoke Friday night, and they asked me to return Sunday night. On the first night I trained slightly over two hundred of his leaders on principles of evangelism in the church. Then on Sunday night I returned to conduct a church service for the entire congregation.

Sunday night before the service began, a gentleman who had been in attendance on Friday night pulled me aside and asked me to go out into the parking lot to his car. "I have something I want to give you," he said.

I had been doing a study on restoration in the Bible. I had been feeling particularly inspired with the topic that God does restore to us what has been taken. So the verses were fresh in my mind, and the concept was rolling around in my head. I knew God was about to start restoring some lost treasures to me. But I never connected my developing thoughts with this little trip to the parking lot.

The gentleman opened the side of his van and said to me, "I own a factory, and we make jackets. I felt the Lord tell me to give you this jacket."

I began thanking him before even seeing it, but when he stretched the jacket toward me, I almost passed out. It was the exact type of jacket that was stolen from me four years earlier. Now call me silly, but I knew that was one of God's signs assuring me that I could count on him restoring everything I had lost.

God Cares about the Small Things

I have no doubt that God cares about the seemingly small issues in our lives. He restores some of them just when we think we can take no more. Truly, he's the God of the restoration of all things.

Let's take a glance at this within the topic of this book. Remember that everyone we correct is dear to God and that his intention is to restore what he or she has lost. Not only are we to correct our friends in the church but also while criticizing we're to spur each other on to growth. Yes, today there's plenty of room to criticize all of us. But the great critic also gives something back that has been lost.

I'm hopeful that you'll take the material of this book and apply it seriously. I know I have since I've been writing it. And I've found many occasions to spur my own growth to be more of a restorative person.

Conclusion

Criticism: Friend or Foe?

I recently watched for the third time a very moving motion picture about a guy named Rudy. Rudy was a student at Notre Dame University in the mid-1970s who wanted above all things to play football for the school. He had a couple of problems, however: He was only five feet tall, and he weighed just over 100 pounds—not exactly the physique for a player in a major collegiate force.

After finally getting on the team, Rudy plodded his way through three seasons seated on the bench. And in practices he was part of what they called "the meat squad"—the guys the big backs practiced running over the top of. Rudy's all-consuming dream was to suit up for just one game. But over four arduous seasons he never got to suit up even once.

One of the most moving scenes of the movie is when he visited the roster on the wall listing those who would suit up. For the fortieth time, he wasn't on it. He broke down into tears and decided to quit the team. The team missed him, however, and his friends on the team encouraged him to come back in the practices.

On Wednesday afternoon he missed the first fifteen minutes of practice but changed his mind and regained his courage after a conversation with the long-time custodian at the stadium. He boldly treaded back onto the practice field, and the entire team applauded him. They loved his determination.

None knew it was the strong correction of the janitor that got him back on the field. As a friend, the stadium custodian rebuffed Rudy for giving up his dreams. He needed a critic that believed in him and he had one in the custodian.

I want those I love to gain courage from the input they receive from me. I want my words to inspire the kind of persistence that led Rudy back on that field. The janitor's criticism was friendly all the way.

One by one the team decided that they wouldn't go onto the field unless Rudy suited up for the game. Coach Dan Devine refused to suit Rudy.

The captain of the team turned in his jersey, asking Devine to give Rudy his spot on the team. Then several linemen followed with the same request. In the movie, Devine's desk was loaded with forty to fifty jerseys from the first-string team.

That Saturday in the great game of Notre Dame against Georgia Tech there was a lot at stake. Both teams were determined to win. Rudy had no hopes of playing but was beaming with joy because he finally got to suit up at least.

Notre Dame took a resounding lead over Georgia Tech, and the opposing team was defeated soundly by the start of the fourth quarter. As the game got down to its final seconds, the team began to clap and chant, "Rudy! Rudy!" and soon all the fans in the Notre Dame stands were also chanting loudly, "Rudy! Rudy!"

The team even forged to another touchdown, against Devine's wishes, so there would be enough time on the clock that Rudy, a defensive non-standout, would have a chance to get into the game. As the crowd chanted, Dan Devine relented and let Rudy into the game.

Rudy played on the kickoff return. He didn't tackle anyone— he just ran down the field. The last play of the game was a final defensive play. When Georgia Tech snapped the ball, Rudy burst through the line and tackled the quarterback. Yes! He got the last tackle! The crowd continued to shout with increasing intensity and volume, "Rudy! Rudy!"

The players of Notre Dame carried Rudy off the field to the chants of the crowd. The postscript of the movie reads, "Not since this date in 1975 has any Notre Dame player been carried off the field."

The touching part of this story is that it's true. The power of the story is that this young man possessed three characteristics. One, he was a learner. Two, he was persistent. And three, he didn't know the word "failure." But there was another turn in this story. He had a loving confronter who forced him to face himself and to rise to meet his dreams.

One of the great friends in my life was writer Jamie Buckingham. Jamie died about ten years ago. I still experience a deep sense of loss when I think of him or pull out one of his books from my shelves.

Jamie helped me work through my first two books. The first was a biography of a mob figure. I'll never forget returning from Jamie's home near Daytona Beach, Florida, with my first three chapters. I've never been able to type very well due to a dyslexic tendency, but I worked and sweated over this text. I felt it was at least a little promising.

I handed the text to Jamie. He pushed it aside, looked at me, and said, "So are you familiar with the Bible verse in Hebrews 12 that says that those whom the Lord loves He chastises—and the one who doesn't get chastised is no more than a 'bastard'?"

I chuckled and responded, "Yes, I'm familiar with the passage."

Jamie went on: "Well, then, you're about to discover that you're not a bastard. Because you're about to get criticized and chastised for as long as you may live as a writer." Then Jamie grabbed the text of my three chapters and pulled a red pen out and gripped it ready for action. I winced by the time he was done with the first three pages—all of them were filled with red marks. The puzzled look on his face caused my heart to drop to the floor.

See? When you're a writer, you don't just put words on a page—you mark up the page with your heart. Every artist knows that whether it's music, writing, or painting, the only way you can do it effectively is to do the work as though it were part of your very being.

I saw that my mentor was ready to point out how deficient I was as a writer. I knew when he was done that I had a long way to go before I would dare call myself a writer.

Finally I asked, "What do you think?"

He leaned back and chuckled and said, "It's terrible. But that's the good part about it."

I responded, *"That's* what's good about it?"

He said, "Yes. All good writing starts off terribly. All good writers have the courage to come out of hiding to be discovered for how far they have to go."

He told me to take out a pad of paper so I could write down twenty mistakes I continually made. And then he handed me the chapters and said, "Now go apply what I just taught you." I spent the next eighteen hours going over the text of these three chapters applying the lessons I had learned and removing any trace of these twenty mistakes.

I wrote most of the night trying to improve my writing. The next morning I got up and took a swim in the ocean. It was like cleansing away the aftertaste of discovering my inadequacies as a writer. Then I got into the car and headed right back to Jamie's home. I handed him my revised three chapters. Once again, he pushed the chapters aside and asked, "Are you familiar with Hebrews chapter 12?"

I replied, "Yes, and I've experienced it thoroughly."

We both laughed. Jamie went through the text this time, making only about a fourth of the original markings he had made before. I again asked him how good it was. He said, "It's a little bit better than terrible now, but that's the good part. Anything worth doing or writing is worth doing poorly at first, but the way to greatness is to have an ear for criticism and to be at heart a life-long learner. I think you're going to make it. I've been testing your ability to receive instruction, and you've done well. So go from here, keep writing and polishing, and in a few weeks we'll go over the text again. I think you'll be surprised how good the book will become.

I completed the text three months later. Jamie and I met, and I handed him the completed twenty-four chapters. This time he didn't give me the Hebrews 12 speech but simply flipped through the chapters reading carefully. When he was finished, he stacked the chapters up neatly and tapped the edges of the paper so that they made a perfect rectangle. Then he looked at me and said, "It is better than I thought it would be."

I asked, "Then does this mean it's good?"

Jamie replied, "No it's not good. It's sort of like Jesus' statement when someone called him good. And Jesus said there was no one good but God. There's no person who is without the need for life-long learning and criticism to grow."

"So how good is it?" I asked again.

He said, "Good enough that quite a few people would probably buy it—but not good enough to get you in the top ten authors in this country. You must keep working at it."

I really miss the friendship I had with Jamie. We shared many laughs. We walked through hard times together. What I loved most about him is that he never backed off helping me to be a better person and to face my own foibles.

I hope this book has given you a good outline to make criticism work well. But even more important than that, I'm most hopeful that many will learn how to give courage to others for their march into what lies ahead for them.

Doug Murren is the director of *Square One Ministries*, a ministry committed to increasing the effectiveness of evangelism in local churches. He was the lead pastor of a congregation in Kirkland, Washington for nearly 20 years and was a pacesetter in the area of outreach, recording 17,000 conversions. Doug is an ordained minister in the Free Methodist denomination, but he has an expansive consulting ministry to all denominations and local churches.

Doug is the author of eleven books.

He and is wife Lori live in Seattle, Washington.

If you would like to receive Doug's weekly free email newsletter write dmurren@square1.org.

You may visit Doug's website for further information at www.square1.org.